REPUBLICS.

REPUBLICS;

OR,

POPULAR GOVERNMENT AN APPOINTMENT OF GOD.

BY THE

REV. JOHN CROWELL, D.D.

"The earth hath he given to the children of men."

PHILADELPHIA:
PRESBYTERIAN BOARD OF PUBLICATION,
No. 1334 CHESTNUT STREET.

Westcott & Thomson,

Stereotypers, Philada.

CONTENTS.

CHAPTER II.

CHAPTER III.

PART III.

THE REPUBLICS OF MODERN TIMES.

CHAPTER I.

CHAPTER II.

CHAPTER III.

THE SUBJECT STATED.

THE Scriptures recognize the right of every established government to the obedience of the people who live under it. This right, they declare, is conferred not by the people, but by God himself. "Let every soul be subject to the higher powers. For there is no power but of God: the powers that be are ordained of God. Whosoever therefore resisteth the power, resisteth the ordinance of God: and they that resist shall receive to themselves condemnation."[1]

These precepts have their place in an inspired and systematic exhibition of Christian doctrine. Concerning obedience to established governments, they are as binding as the doctrine of justification by faith is with reference to the way of salvation. The obedience they require is not absolute or unconditional, but has limits and laws. The word of God supplies light by which the limits may be defined and the laws studied.

The government existing when these precepts were enjoined on Christians was a monarchy—a despotism. It had extended its dominion by conquest, crushing

[1] Romans xiii. 1, 2.

other governments or absorbing them into its own. It was administered not by a wise and humane ruler, but by a tyrant; by Nero, not Trajan. Yet do the laws of Christianity declare that even such a government is clothed with lawful authority by God himself, and that resistance to *that* is rebellion against him.

From these positive commands *to obey a monarchy* when established as the actual government, the inference has been drawn that God approves and appoints monarchy as, of right, the form of government for mankind.

This inference has acquired increased plausibility from the fact that the governments existing during the whole period with which Scripture history is conversant were, with few exceptions, monarchies; consequently, the Bible gives prominence and splendor to the actions of kings. Patriarchs, prophets, apostles, even Christ himself, were called before them, addressed them by their titles, acknowledged their authority and submitted to it. The Saviour stood before the imperial governor as before one to whom power from above had been given. The apostle of the Gentiles appealed to Cæsar's judgment-seat as a tribunal "where he *ought* to be judged." Indeed, the whole Bible has something regal in its tone, caused by its frequent recognition of the established governments of kings. Thus it has the more easily happened that the doctrine of the divine right of kings, maintained as if sanctioned by the Bible, has contributed in no small degree and with no transient influence to the stability of their thrones. While their persons have been rendered splendid with gems and purple, and secure by the locked array of armed men, they have attained sacredness also from the awful words, "*Ex Dei gratiâ.*"

In opposition to this doctrine we propose to show that republican governments are a gift from God, and to accomplish our object shall adduce—

I. The Republic of the Hebrew State.

II. The Republics of the Christian Church.

III. The Republics in Church and State resulting from the diffusion of Christianity in modern times.

PART I.

The Republic of the Hebrew State.

"When the Most High divided unto the nations their inheritance he set their bounds according to the number of the children of Israel."

REPUBLICS.

CHAPTER I.

THE REPUBLIC FOUNDED.

"I will make of thee a great nation."

Section 1.—Primitive Liberty among Men.

"Let them have dominion over all the earth."

SCRIPTURE history clearly shows that in the re-settlement of the earth after the flood no kingly governments received the sanction of God.

That history begins with *the people* as the earthly source of power. It sets them before us as individuals, families, nations. "These are the families of the sons of Noah, after their generation, in their nations; and by these were the nations divided in the earth after the flood."[1] It calls them "the children of men," and says of them: "The people is one;" "they have all one language;" "this they begin to do; and nothing will be restrained from them which they have imagined to do."[2]

[1] Gen. x. 32. [2] Gen. xi. 5, 6.

This language is descriptive of democratic sovereignty, union and energy, and, because these attributes were unrestrained by law, of violence too.

God broke up the vast democracy into pieces by confounding their language. The fragments, however, as they fell from his hand, were democratic still. He appointed no king over them. After their division the people are described as scattered abroad, as before, in tribes, according to their descent.

At this point in their history individuals among them began to usurp power over them. The transition from freedom to despotism is sharply defined in the sacred narrative, and the unauthorized character of the process is positively declared.

Nimrod—whose name signifies "a rebel," an apostate—is stigmatized as the leader in the acquisition of greatness by the selfish, violent exercise of force. It is said of him that "he began to be a mighty one in the earth," and "was a mighty hunter in the face of Jehovah."[1]

By many of the best interpreters of Scripture, both ancient and modern, the epithet "*hunter*" has been regarded as representing chiefly Nimrod's conduct toward men. "The establishment of an

[1] Gen. x. 8, 9.

empire, transforming the patriarchal governments into one monarchy, is not to be thought of as happening without force. The chase of the animals was for Nimrod and his companions a training for war, a preparatory exercise, the bridge of transition to the hunting and subjugation of men."[1]

"Proud Nimrod first the bloody chase began—
A mighty hunter, and his prey was man."

"He did this 'in the face of Jehovah'—that is, presumptuously and in defiance of divine authority. It was God's design that the earth should be settled in tribes and nations under popular forms of government, and Nimrod's sin consisted in contravening the divine counsel and in laying the foundation, by means of violent usurpation, of that species of dominion—since distinguished by the names 'kingdoms,' 'empires,' 'monarchies'—by which the great mass of mankind have been doomed to ignorance and held in bondage."[2]

His example was rapidly imitated, and in proportion as men succeeded in usurping power they were said to be "even as Nimrod, the mighty hunter, in the face of Jehovah."

In him also we read the beginning of the lesson

[1] Lange in loc. [2] Bush's Notes.

that the corruption of divine worship and the destruction of human liberty go hand in hand together.

Josephus says of him "that he gradually changed the government into tyranny, seeing no other way of turning men from the fear of God but to bring them to a constant dependence on his own power." The Targum of Jerusalem also charges him with saying to those around him, "Depart from the religion of Shem and cleave unto the institutes of Nimrod."

Through all ages the opportunity to learn this lesson has been prolonged. Both Scripture and secular history show *that wherever religion was corrupted there monarchies arose.*

"The beginning of his kingdom was Babel."[1] This being the record at the opening of the Scriptures, at the close of the Old Testament the same Babylon is exhibited in all the grandeur and pride of its oppressions over men. The Prophets, from Isaiah to Daniel, foretell its fall, and history attests the fulfillment of their words, beginning the very night in which the trembling Belshazzar heard his doom, and completed in distant times. And at the close of the New Testament we find the same great

[1] Gen. x. 10.

city employed as the symbol to represent the mighty spiritual despotism which, building itself up on its corruptions of the word of God, arrogates dominion over all the earth; over Church and State; over the body, mind and soul; life and death; hell and heaven. Its fall is there foretold in majestic terms, compared with which the doom of the literal city seems only a still, small voice.

Such are the lines which the Scriptures run across the ages, at once from Paradise lost to Paradise regained, and from Babel to the bottomless pit. Along these lines extends the course of human governments which we seek to trace.

Sect. 2.—Abraham and his Descendants.

"Unto a land that I will show thee."

From the midst of the spreading idolatry and rising monarchy Abraham was called forth by the voice of God.

His mission was the starting-point of a divine plan for the benefit of mankind which has ever since been in progress, and is designed to transform the religious and civil condition of the whole world. "In thee shall all the families of the earth be blessed."[1]

[1] Gen. xii. 3.

This promise includes both spiritual and temporal blessing—the one of supreme and everlasting importance, the other less only than that, and vitally connected with it. At present we are concerned directly with the temporal blessing rather than the spiritual, and with one department only of that, viz.: THE REPUBLICAN CIVIL GOVERNMENT CONFERRED, AS A GIFT FROM GOD, ON THE CHILDREN OF ABRAHAM.

Abraham and his immediate descendants governed their families, for they were, as yet, few in number, and the simple principles of patriarchal rule were sufficient for their wants. But at the termination of their long sojourn in Egypt they had so mightily increased that a national government was required. As it was appointed by God himself, we are especially interested in ascertaining what its form and character were.

We must not look for it in its completeness until the settlement of the people in the promised land, yet from the beginning of God's interposition in their behalf the nature of the government began to appear.

Here is the place to hold up to view three important principles which were clearly established before the promised land was reached.

1. First of all, it was in their behalf, *as a people, that God interposed.* "Their cry came up unto him." He said to Moses concerning them: "I have seen the affliction of *my people*, have heard their cry, and am come down to deliver them."[1] His message to Pharaoh was, "Let *my people* go."[2] He brought them out of Egypt as "the hosts of the Lord." Through the wilderness his providence was over them *as a people*, and on the margin of the promised land the final benediction of Moses upon them was, "Happy art thou, *O people* saved by the Lord."[3]

In this opening of their history we see God recognizing the children of Israel as a nation. All his treatment of them warrants and requires the inference that in their political relations he regarded them as the depositary of power, subject only to himself.

2. This being so, let us take notice, secondly, *that no king was set over them*, either by the direct appointment of God or by their own choice approved by him.

Moses was their leader, appointed of God and clothed with great authority. But he was not a king. He wore no crown, was not arrayed in

[1] Ex. ii. 23; iii. 6. [2] Ex. v. 1. [3] Deut. xxxiii. 29.

royal robes and was not surrounded with household troops or prætorian guards. Not in name or reality, not in form or substance, was there anything regal in the position that he held. The people were not his vassals or even his army. He was their leader, and, in the turbulent exercise of their democratic will, they threatened to take his life or to choose a captain and march away. In all such emergencies his authority, and even his life, depended entirely on God. A rod was his only weapon, a pillar of cloud and fire his only shield.

3. It is clear that, when the foundations of civil government for Israel were laid, *the principle of hereditary succession to its highest office was rejected.* Had it been adopted, the government would have grown into a monarchy, whatever it might have been at the beginning, but, by the rejection of it, God's purpose to guard against such growth was declared.

The authority with which Moses was clothed was temporary and the work assigned him as definite as it was difficult and grand. In its political aspects it included the deliverance of the people from Egypt, their guidance through the wilderness and establishment in Canaan. As he was to die, according to the revealed purpose of God, before the accomplishment of the last division of the work, a successor to his high office must eventually be appointed.

Moses had sons; they were with their father in the camp; but they make no figure in the history. They were not raised to any office or clothed with any privilege on account of their relationship to the leader of the people. They are never mentioned in the subsequent history until the time of David, when it is recorded that their descendants continued in an honorable position among the Levites, the lower grade of the priesthood to which they were destined by their birth.[1] It is consequently certain that the family of Moses inherited from him *no political rank.* This fact, in itself striking, becomes doubly so when contrasted with the hereditary spiritual office which, for the accomplishment of a special object, was conferred on the sons of Aaron.

But, while Moses permitted his sons to live undistinguished in the camp, soon after the departure

[1] "Of the Levites, . . . Shebuel the son of Gershom, the son of Moses, was ruler of the treasures. And his brethren by Eliezer . . . were over all the treasures of the dedicated things." 1 Chron. xxvi. 20–28.

from Egypt he chose Joshua, a young man of another tribe, to be the military leader, and in all things, during the forty years, placed him near himself in confidential relations and second in active influence. Thus he who had been designated by divine appointment to succeed Moses became qualified for all his duties. And as the time for the death of the great leader drew nigh, he called Joshua, and by divine command, in the sight of all Israel, solemnly invested him with the office.

When Joshua had finished his work of leading Israel into Canaan and his time came to die, he also was not succeeded in office by his son.

Thus signally was the principle of hereditary succession refused a place in the corner-stone of the Hebrew state. And as, through many generations, we trace the influence of this principle wherever it has been admitted into human governments, as we learn the oppression it has caused and the blood it has shed, the wisdom of God in rejecting it conspicuously appears.

CHAPTER II.

THE REPUBLIC ESTABLISHED.

"Go in and possess the land."

THE Hebrews, as we have shown, moved forward to the possession of Canaan, with three important facts established concerning their civil institutions, viz.: that God had recognized them as a people by his interposition in their behalf; that no king had been set over them either by divine authority or their own choice; and that they were not to be subjected to hereditary rule.

On the foundation thus laid a republic was now to be reared. That this was done we shall show by establishing the following propositions:

1. That by the gift and division of the land republican institutions were secured.

2. That the revealed religion was adopted by the voluntary choice of the people.

3. That there was a republican administration of the laws.

Sect. 1.—The Gift and Division of the Land.

"He divideth it unto them by lot."

God is the sovereign owner of the soil, from whom all titles to it are derived. His sovereignty in it, arising from actual creation, is absolute and perpetual. He exercises it over all the lands of the earth, bestowing them on the nations according to his will. "God hath made of one blood all nations of men for to dwell on all the face of the earth, and hath determined the times before appointed, and the bounds of their habitation."[1]

In his covenant with Abraham he promised the land of Canaan to his descendants: "Unto thy seed have I given this land, from the river of Egypt unto the great river, the river Euphrates."[2] This promise was renewed to Moses soon after the deliverance from Egypt: "I will set thy bounds from the Red Sea to the sea of the Philistines, and from the desert unto the river."[3] It was repeated again at the expiration of forty years to the new generation who were to enter the land: "Every place whereon the soles of your feet shall tread shall be yours, from the wilderness and Lebanon, from the river Euphrates to the utmost sea."[4] It was re-

[1] Acts xvii. 26. [2] Gen. xv. 18.
[3] Ex. xxiii. 31. [4] Deut. xi. 24.

newed finally and in similar terms to Joshua on the banks of the Jordan, and the accomplishment of it was committed to him.[1]

By this gift of the land to the people at large as their common country, God constituted them a nation; AND BY CONFERRING THE OWNERSHIP OF A PORTION OF THE LAND ON EVERY MAN HE CONSTITUTED THEM A REPUBLICAN NATION.

Let us attend carefully to this great fact in the history of God's dealings with Israel. According to his command, the land of Canaan—his gift to the nation—was apportioned to each tribe, to each family, to each individual, and by this arrangement, we repeat, republican institutions were secured.

In order to understand the effect on the government and laws of the ownership of the land by all the people, let us contrast it with "the feudal system" which was introduced into modern Europe by the Northern nations.

The foundation of that system was this: "Large districts of conquered territory were allotted by the conquering general to the superior officers of the army, and by them dealt out again in smaller parcels to the inferior officers and most deserving soldiers. These allotments were subject to the

[1] Josh. i. 4.

condition that the possessor should do service, both at home and in the wars, to him by whom they were given, for which purpose he took the oath of fealty, and in case of the breach of this condition and oath, by not performing the stipulated service or by deserting the lord in battle, the lands were again to revert to him who granted them."

This one principle bound all the people to one man as their sovereign, lord and king, and to others in subordination to him, thus establishing a regal and aristocratic government.

The feudal system was adopted in other countries besides those into which it was introduced by conquest. "Most, if not all, of the princes of Europe thought it necessary to enter into the same or a similar plan. For whereas, before, the possessions of their subjects were wholly independent and held of no superior at all, now they parceled out their royal territories, *or persuaded their subjects to surrender up and retake their own landed property under the like feudal obligations of military fealty.* And thus, in the compass of a very few years, the feudal constitution, or the doctrine of tenure, extended itself all over the Western world."

As the introduction of the system into conquered

countries built up monarchical and aristocratic institutions of a solid and vigorous nature, so its voluntary adoption produced similar results in strengthening existing kings and in altering the whole fabric of institutions and laws. "The alteration of landed property in so very material a point necessarily drew after it an alteration of laws and customs, so that the feudal laws soon drove out the Roman, which had hitherto universally obtained, but now became for many centuries lost and forgotten, and Italy itself submitted to the laws of the Lombards, ruthless, fierce and savage as they were."

The whole effect of the feudal system was witnessed in England, where it was introduced by William the Conqueror, partly by bestowing the forfeited lands of the English who had fallen in battle on his Norman followers, and partly by persuading his English subjects "to submit their lands to the yoke of military tenure, to become his vassals and do homage to his person." "In consequence of this change it became a fundamental maxim and necessary principle of English tenures (though in reality a mere fiction) that the king is the universal lord and original proprietor of all the lands in his kingdom, and that no man doth or can possess any part of it but what has mediately or immediately been derived as a gift from him to be held upon feudal services. For this being the case in pure, original proper feuds, other nations who adopted this system were obliged to act on the same supposition, as a substruction and foundation of their new polity, though the fact was indeed far otherwise." "Thus were introduced not only the vigorous doctrines which prevailed in the duchy of Normandy, but also such fruits and dependencies, such hardships and services, as were never known to other nations, as if the English had in fact, as well as theory, owed everything they had to the bounty of their sovereign lord."[1]

And as a result of the same system, the structure of English liberty even to this day retains the appearance either of violence, as if the people had wrested from the king a portion of his prerogative, or of vassalage, as if on their bended knee they had received from him a royal boon; whereas all that they have acquired, either by force or favor, is only the recovery of a part of what was originally their own.

From this historical view (which has been intentionally given chiefly in well-known language

[1] Blackstone's Commentaries.

of acknowledged authority) it appears that the condition of servitude attached to the tenure of landed property necessarily involves subjection to a monarch and to others under him, and turns all laws and customs into chains. And by parity of reasoning we conclude that, on the contrary, where, at the organization of a state, there is an ownership of the land by the people entirely independent of any human superior, there will be exemption from kingly and aristocratic rule. The possessor of the land is, so far as it and his own person are concerned, a sovereign on his own domain. He is subject to God because from him he holds both his own being and the land on which he dwells. But with reference to his own conduct and interest he is independent of *men.* Where *all* the people possess this ownership they are all, as individuals, independent of other men, and as they are connected together in a common country, with mutual and interlocked interests, a "commonwealth," a REPUBLIC, necessarily exists.

To apply this reasoning to the case before us. If, after the conquest of Canaan, Joshua, as the commanding general, had apportioned the land as a grant for himself to his superior officers, and they had subdivided it among the inferior officers and soldiers, a government of king, lords and commons would have have been established. Had this division been made by God's command, then the king and his nobles would have reigned "by divine right." But as, on the contrary, the land—the gift of God to all the people—was divided among them all, republican institutions were thereby established.

If Joshua had himself devised the plan, he would have been entitled to high praise for equity and wisdom, and the Hebrew republic, however worthy of imitation, would have been a human institution. But the plan of dividing a portion to every man was as much from God as the land itself was his gift. All the persons to be entrusted with making the division he had appointed by name before the conquest, and on republican principles—one from each tribe, together with Joshua, the civil and military ruler, and Eleazar, the high priest. He had directed the division to be made by lot, "the whole disposing of which was of himself."

It is therefore clear that the Hebrew republic was an appointment of God. Consequently for republican government, wherever established, we may adduce his sanction, and may point to the Bible as at least one of the sources whence the model of such a government has been derived.

Sect. 2.—The Adoption of Religion by the People.

"Choose you whom ye will serve."

The republican character of the Hebrew government appears also in the fact that the question of adopting the revealed religion was determined by the free choice of the people.

We certainly do not maintain that the consent of men is necessary in order to establish the authority of God over them. On the contrary, his absolute sovereignty is a necessary inference from their entire dependence. His right to their service and worship is independent alike of their consent or refusal. But he desires only voluntary service. Therefore his right to demand it implies the right of men to yield it. His right to prescribe religion implies their right to adopt it.

When a monarchy is established the king in general arrogates to himself the power of imposing religion on his subjects by his royal edict. Darius, for example, did so. When convinced by the deliverance of Daniel that Jehovah was the living God, he "wrote unto all people, nations and languages that dwell in all the earth, '*I make a decree that in every dominion of my kingdom men tremble and fear before the God of Daniel.'"*[1] This single instance fairly represents the great volume of royal proclamations on the subject of religion, whether false or true. But where the people have the power of acting on the subject for themselves, this department of their government is manifestly republican.

Among the Hebrews this was the fact. God revealed his law to them as a nation. His words were spoken to the assembled multitude, demanding obedience from every man: "*Thou* shalt have no other gods before me." The evidence that it was from him was addressed publicly to them all. Thus declared and proved, it was binding on them; but the question whether they would receive it was between them and God. The adoption of it was to be their own voluntary act.

Accordingly, after their settlement in Canaan, the subject was submitted to them in a public assembly, the proceedings at which are recorded in the book of Joshua.[2] These we commonly regard as a narrative concerning an important religious duty, but they are not less significant as recording the exercise of a high civil privilege by a free

[1] Dan. vi. 25, 26. [2] Chapter xxiv.

people. They prove that there was no decree issued imposing the worship of God on them, but that, all civil authority over religious affairs being disclaimed, the right of every man to judge and act for himself was recognized, the civil magistrate having simply the same right as every other man: "*Choose you whom ye will serve; as for me and my house, we will serve the Lord.*"

This choice the people deliberately made, saying, THE LORD OUR GOD WILL WE SERVE, AND HIS VOICE WILL WE OBEY. And thus was a covenant entered into between God and the people, without the intervention of king or ruler, by virtue of which the law revealed by him and adopted by them became the recognized religion of the land.

Sect. 3.—The Republican Administration of the Laws.

"*He gave them judges.*"

The office which Moses and Joshua successively held, though dictatorial in some respects, was only temporary, having been appointed to extend from the deliverance of the people out of Egypt to their establishment in the promised land. The later portion of this period covered all the life of Joshua, and at his death a most decisive difference appears between the close of his official career and that of Moses.

Moses had assembled the people, announced to them his approaching death, and in their presence solemnly transferred his authority to Joshua. The transfer, made by divine command, was publicly confirmed with the symbol of the divine presence. But nothing like this occurred at the end of Joshua's life. No successor to him was inaugurated, nominated or provided. When he died his office expired, and the next chapter of the history introduces an entire change in the administration of public affairs. "After the death of Joshua the children of Israel asked the Lord, Who shall go up for us against the Canaanites?"[1] They stood before God a nation without an earthly head, exercising their sovereignty in subjection only to him. Their subsequent history down to the old age of Samuel presents a continued exhibition of popular liberty almost without restraint: "In those days there was no king in Israel: every man did that which was right in his own eyes."[2]

Yet they were not without provision for the administration of the laws. At a very early period after the departure from Egypt, Moses had

[1] Book of Judges, first verse. [2] Ibid., last verse.

"chosen from all Israel able men, who feared God and hated covetousness, to be rulers over thousands, hundreds, fifties and tens."[1] Their office was to judge the people at all times; when any matter arose between man and man they declared and applied the statutes and laws appropriate to the case. The smaller causes they decided themselves, the harder they referred to Moses.

Here is the outline of a system of ascending courts not unlike that which is now so prominent in the United States, and in which is lodged so much of the government that is exercised over the people "at all times." And the qualifications which Moses required are the very ones which the experience of all ages since has demanded. Let the judges of lower and higher jurisdiction among us, or any people where liberty is guaranteed by the laws, be ABLE MEN, HATING COVETOUSNESS AND FEARING GOD, and we are as safe as human government can make us. Let them, as a class and continuously, be destitute of these qualifications, and the choice of anarchy or despotism would soon be upon us.

This reference to our own country is made not so much for the sake of sounding a warning as for

[1] Ex. xviii. 21-26.

throwing the light of our institutions on those of the Hebrews. Since among us adequate provision is made for the usual purposes of internal government by the general establishment of legal tribunals, we may understand the nature and value of the similar provision made by Moses.

These magistrates were continued among the people. Moses by divine authority directed that they should be established through all the cities, towns and districts of the promised land: "Judges and officers shalt thou make thee in all thy gates, which the Lord thy God giveth thee throughout thy tribes; and these shall judge the people with just judgment."[1]

In the assembly called by Joshua, all Israel, with their "elders," "heads," "officers" and "judges," were present. At a later period the "governors of Israel," "the men of laws," rallied around Deborah.[2] And from the language employed by Moses—judges and officers *shalt thou make thee*—it is plain that the people were in some way to exercise their choice in the appointment.

A supreme officer having authority over all the land was appointed from time to time. He too was a judge to *execute* the laws, not a king to *impose* them.

[1] Deut. xvi. 18. [2] Judges v. 9. חוֹקְקֵי.

The manner of this appointment is not always declared. In general it is said: "The Lord raised up judges." Sometimes, perhaps, we may infer only that his providence fitted them for the crisis and made it necessary for them to act. Sometimes, certainly, his positive command called them to the post; always the manifest exercise of his power gave them success. Sometimes, at least, popular choice was mingled with divine appointment, as in the case of Jephthah, to whom the elders of Gilead promised that if he would lead them against their enemies he should be their head. He consented, "and the people made him head and captain over them." His authority, having begun in this way, was extended over all Israel.[1]

Perhaps, by adopting or permitting these various modes, God was training the people for the safe exercise of the highest but most perilous act of sovereignty—the choice, at frequently-recurring intervals, of a supreme executive officer for all the land.

[1] Judg. xi. 11; xii. 7.

CHAPTER III.

THE REPUBLIC OVERTHROWN.

"Nay, but we will have a king."

IF we would attain correct ideas concerning the practical operation of the Hebrew republic, we must remember that the experiment was new and the work difficult.

In the past were no precedents to which the rising nation might appeal, and in the present no examples by which it might be instructed and cheered. The people also who were to compose the nation had been rescued from bondage only forty years before. All their ideas of government had been formed under a grievous despotism upheld by brutal force. During their sojourn in the wilderness the older men, whose opinions and habits, we must suppose, were hopelessly fixed, gradually died. The new generation, to whom the experiment was to be entrusted, were subjected to constant discipline that they might be qualified for the work. Yet as they were destitute of practical experience (without which theoretical instruction is at best insufficient), we should not be surprised that many difficulties proved formidable and many temptations overpowering. It was to be expected that their liberty would not be unmingled with turbulence, and that commotion, strife and violence would not be unknown. These are parts of the first cost which must be paid for liberty. That it was paid by Israel is plain enough from their annals.

Yet even at the beginning the advantages greatly overbalanced the evils; the periods of tranquillity were much longer than those of violence and misrule. For here, as in all history, we must remember that, while war, tumult and calamity are spread out as warnings on the page, prosperous and quiet times are unnoticed or have only a line devoted to them, recording that the land had rest forty or even eighty years. It is the reef or the headland that is marked by the lighthouse, but the broad expanse of open sea "retains no furrow from the keels" that glide safely through it. And, in the progress of the experiment, the chief evils that arose are not to be attributed to the form of government or to perils peculiar to civil affairs. They sprang from the moral corruption of the people impelling them to violate first their duties to God and then their obligations to man. It was not until religion was prostrated that liberty became licentiousness and civil war desolated the land.

We now approach the period when the divinely-given government of the Hebrews was overthrown by their own hands.

Their first decided movement toward having a king was occasioned by Gideon's splendid victories over Midian. In the delirium of their joy they thrust the crown on his acceptance for himself and his sons for ever: "Rule thou over us, both thou and thy son and thy son's son also, for thou hast delivered us from Midian." He refused the offer sincerely and resolutely: "I will not rule over you, neither shall my son. The Lord alone shall rule over you."[1] The Lord alone is Sovereign over all.

By this refusal Gideon placed his name among the few of earth's noblest ones who with similar opportunities have scorned to destroy the liberties they had saved. As judge over the people he continued to be their benefactor. The Midianites lifted up their heads no more, and the land was in

[1] Judg. viii. 22–28.

quietness forty years. Yet in all his wisdom and honor "a little folly" appeared. Refusing the crown, he asked for the gold and spoils, and, making an ephod from them as a memorial of his victories, hung it up in his native city. By this act of vanity he stimulated the passion of the people for idolatrous worship and spread a snare for himself and his house. As soon as he was dead, all restraint being removed, the people rushed madly back to the worship of Baal.

Then Abimelech, the least honored of Gideon's sons, seized the royal power. He inaugurated his usurpation with the murder of all his brethren except the youngest, who in his flight hurled back on him the bitter sarcasm that when the olive, the fig and the vine had declined being king over the trees the bramble took them under its shade. His reign was short and troubled. After three years revolt was raised against him, and in the attempt to subdue it, just as success seemed sure, he fell mortally wounded by a woman's hand.

By his defeat and death the introduction of royalty was for the time delayed. The yoke was not to be fastened on the people by treachery or force, but by their own voluntary choice.

The revolution was accomplished one hundred

and forty years after, in the old age of Samuel the prophet. He had himself judged Israel many years with great fidelity and zeal, but in his old age he made his sons judges in his stead. By this act, so strangely in contrast with the bright record of his whole life, he committed the double wrong of introducing hereditary succession and of appointing wicked men. His sons walked not in his ways, but turned aside after lucre, took bribes and perverted judgment.

Seizing the pretext offered by their misrule, the people demanded "a king to judge them *like all the nations.*"

Samuel was displeased, and disposed to resist. He, however, referred the application to God. His answer was: "*Hearken to the voice of the people; yet protest solemnly to them, and show them the manner of the king that shall reign over them.*"

The voice of the people is to prevail. They have had the right conferred on them of choosing their own form of government. If they are unwise or even wicked in their choice, there is no right of resisting it by force vested anywhere on earth. A solemn protest is "the last argument" to which a republican ruler or a minority ought to resort against the voice of the nation itself, when that is certainly known and has been legally expressed.

Moses had foretold that the people would some day choose a king, and, without condemning or sanctioning their course, contented himself with prescribing qualifications which the king must possess and laws which he must obey: "When thou shalt say, '*I will set a king over me like as all the nations that are about me,*' thou shalt in any wise set him over thee whom the Lord shall choose."[1]

The protest which God by the prophet entered against their choice graphically described the transition from republican to monarchical government. The personal liberty of the citizens would be sacrificed, the security of their families invaded and their rights of property trampled under foot. Their independence would be changed to vassalage, *as if* the king had been the original grantor of all their privileges and possessions.

We often strive to conjecture what would have been the result on the *religion* of mankind if the Hebrews had remained true to their mission.

God gave them his law and established them in a central position, that the nations might behold the

[1] Deut. xvii. 14.

light and finally come to it. But they themselves fell into the idolatry of the nations instead of adhering to the true religion which distinguished them from all, and the preservation of which was the chief design of all the restrictions and peculiarities imposed on them. Consequently, God's purpose to make them a blessing to mankind was interfered with and delayed.

We may also in some measure perceive what might have been the influence exerted on the *civil government* of other nations had the Hebrews maintained their own. Its light would have shone on the monarchies which clustered around Palestine as the spectators in an amphitheatre around the stage, and the results produced by American institutions in causing monarchs to tremble on their thrones might have been witnessed at that early day.

But instead of maintaining at all hazards their republican singularity, which was their high privilege and glory, UNTIL THE NATIONS BECAME LIKE THEM, they insisted on having a king, THAT THEY "MIGHT BE LIKE THE NATIONS." Thus with their own hand they hurled to the dust that divinely-kindled torch of which they had been chosen to be the first bearers. The quenching of its glorious light involved them and the world in darkness.

Henceforward the government over them remained a monarchy, with some temporary variations of form, until the remnant of the nation was scattered by the Romans—a period of nearly twelve hundred years.

During those long centuries of moral gloom the Eastern empires rose, flourished and fell; the popular institutions of Greece struggled into existence, shone with splendid but transient lustre, and sank in the empire of Philip and Alexander; the kings of Rome reigned and were expelled; the struggle between the people and the nobles (who had derived their privileges from the kings) advanced with varying fortune for a time, but ended at length in the empire of Augustus, which, beginning about the birth of Christ, was universal over the principal countries of the world.

Yet let us not imagine that the cause of human liberty was lost. Under all the dazzling exterior of imperial power, the principles of Roman, Greek and Hebrew citizenship, seemingly overwhelmed, continued to exist, incapable of being destroyed. Brought near together by outward pressure they coalesced into one, as the body, mind and soul of liberty, which, when inspired with new life from Heaven, would go forth through all lands to make men free.

The workings of this new life it is our part in some slight measure to unfold.

PART II.

The Republics of the Christian Church.

"A little one shall become a thousand."

CHAPTER I.

THE PEOPLE AWAKENED.

"Proclaim liberty throughout the land."

WHEN the apparent failure of the first experiment in establishing republican government was complete, the fullness of time had arrived for entering on the second.

How was it commenced? Not by clearing Palestine or any other land of its inhabitants that there might be room for the erection of new institutions; not by overthrowing any established government that the fabric might rise on its ruins; but while the existing civil governments remained outwardly undisturbed, WITHIN THEM REPUBLICAN RELIGIOUS INSTITUTIONS WERE SILENTLY PLANTED.

This was accomplished by the coming of the Son of God into the world as the Saviour of men. While his highest design concerning them was to secure their eternal welfare, his gospel necessarily affected them also in this life. Our present inquiry is into its influence on their temporal condition only as that is determined by religion and government.

Beginning with religion, it revealed its truths and taught that, with respect to them, men are independent of human authority and responsible only to God. This great fact established, its transforming power over civil government was sure. Men cannot be free in religion without, sooner or later, becoming free also in the state.

As in the primitive history of the world the introduction of false religion had built up despotism on the ruins of liberty, so the restoration of true religion began at once to soften the despotism, and in the future of history is destined to overturn the throne.

Sect. 1.—Religion Separated from the State.

"Unto God the things that are God's."

The Son of God appeared as a teacher on earth in the midst of a despotic government that exercised dominion over all things pertaining to human life and destiny. Especially must we take notice that it made no distinction between civil and religious affairs. It made none, because it knew none. Religion was simply a part of the state, and therefore subject to human law equally with war or commerce.

The Saviour, with unerring accuracy, exposed the falseness of this view. The authority of the rulers over civil affairs he did not oppose. Concerning it he pronounced no opinion except to declare that they, at least, who recognized it in any matters pertaining to it should obey it in all.

In making this decision he drew for all coming time the line of separation between the state and religion. RENDER UNTO CÆSAR THE THINGS THAT ARE CÆSAR'S, AND UNTO GOD THE THINGS THAT ARE GOD'S.

And, in accordance with his own decision, he utterly disregarded Cæsar's claim to authority over things belonging to God. He knew that it had no foundation except in assumption and was maintained only by force. Consequently, he did not go to the civil authority for permission or privilege—nor would he plead before it when arraigned—concerning any things pertaining to his mission as a prophet from God.

On the contrary, he gathered the people around him and taught them, as a right which he of himself possessed, and to which they had an equal right to respond. He selected messengers also to proclaim his religion, and commanded them to make it known to every creature in all the world. By these acts he asserted that, with respect to religion, his disciples and mankind were of right independent of all civil government.

Power to restrict and silence them he knew existed. It was everywhere around them. It always had its hand on them. It might arrest, imprison, scourge them, and put them to death. Of this he warned them, yet gave them no sword for their own defence. On the contrary, he strictly forbade their using the sword. Their own discretion, argument, flight, suffering and his mediatorial care were all the resources he allowed them against the wildest fury of absolute power. But the *right* of the civil government to arrest or hinder them the Saviour ignored as a nullity. They were to go forth everywhere, obedient to him as their sovereign Lord in religious things, and so far independent of men. And their right to do so was finally to prevail over all opposing power.

This separation of religion from civil government was (as we have said) contrary to the theory and practice of mankind at the time it was announced. The Saviour was the only being on earth who then perfectly understood it. Against it human power, thought and prejudice were at once arrayed. In the conflict religion sometimes seemed overwhelmed by the persecution of hostile governments; often it has been almost destroyed by the assumed authority of patronizing rulers. Every step of advance has been a victory won by endurance or bought with disaster. The conflict yet rages in some places with different weapons, but as fiercely as before. Even now decisive struggles seem to be at hand.

But so far as the independence of mankind in religion has been established, or is about to be, the boasted progress of modern times consists in receiving that which was proclaimed at the beginning as the starting-point of revelation in the world.

Sect. 2.—The Principles of Christianity Diffused.

"The common people heard him gladly."

The Saviour, as the spring of his influence on earth, WENT ABOUT AMONG THE MASSES OF THE PEOPLE. In every part of Palestine he gathered them around him and addressed his teaching mainly to them. He directed his disciples to pursue the same course, addressing not kings as such, or nobles, or literary men, or privileged classes of any kind, but the human race and every individual belonging to it. While he designed to reach all, he began not at the highest, but the lowest. "To the poor the gospel was preached." "The common people heard him gladly." As one who would kindle a fire places his spark beneath the fuel, not on the top, so Christ, having "come to send fire on the earth," kindled it in the substratum of society.

His mission and doctrine were pre-eminently adapted to awaken mankind, to reach each individual man as a man, and make him feel that he possessed in himself essential importance and dignity, whatever his condition might be and wherever the bounds of his habitation had been assigned.

Let us glance at some of the great facts and principles which were combined to produce this effect.

1. Jesus Christ the Son of God became man, and that not among kings and nobles, but in the lowliest condition. His humiliation, while it was especially designed to "perfect" him in bringing many to eternal glory, also enabled him to exalt those who were oppressed in this life. What other consideration could so

thrill the bosom of man, awaken his faculties and brace his spirit? Wherever he was free to go forth among the works of God he might find, indeed, much to assure him of the importance that belonged to him in the judgment and by the gift of his Creator, who, amidst such glorious handiwork, had been mindful of *him*, consulting his pleasure, providing for his wants, making him capable of "considering the heavens" with thought profound, and assigning him "dominion over all the earth." But when in the prison-house into which the lordly ones of his fellow-men had thrust him, and where he was slumbering beneath the pressure of arbitrary power, the Son of God stood by his side clothed in a manhood like his own and not ashamed to call him brother, then did he rise up quickly, the chains fell from his hands, the iron gate opened before him and he went forth in his strength. His spirit was stirred within him by the mighty truth that to a nature which had been taken by his Creater on himself there belonged a dignity which no external grandeur could confer, and no transient poverty or oppression take away.

2. The Saviour appealed to every man AS HAVING A CONSCIENCE CAPABLE OF DISTINGUISH-

ING BETWEEN RIGHT AND WRONG AND OF DISCERNING THE CLAIMS OF TRUTH.

This, he declared, was the pre-eminent endowment of human nature. He charged every man to adhere to it against all opposing authority and through the severest suffering, assuring him that in such a struggle God would be on his side against all the world.

One thus endowed and charged with a work so arduous and grand must possess great dignity in the scale of being, and in proportion as his conscience was obeyed and his work performed would that dignity be asserted and maintained.

3. JESUS CHRIST REVEALED A JUDGMENT TO COME AT WHICH EVERY MAN MUST APPEAR AND RENDER AN ACCOUNT OF HIMSELF TO GOD.

Both small and great, the poor and the rich, the weak and the strong, the bond and the free, would stand together at that day. They who sinned in comparative ignorance would be held without excuse so far as they knew or might have known their duty; and they who enjoyed clearer light would have the more required of them, and be visited, if transgressors, with a heavier doom.

He who was on his way to such a judgment-seat, and for whose trial the great white throne would be set in heaven, possessed an essential dignity that could not be alienated or lost, whether he were clothed in rags or purple, whether he wore a yoke on his neck or a crown on his head. Destined to a personal account amidst the millions that would surround the throne, he should not be disregarded on earth merely because he was one of a mass. Assured of justice at the bar of God, he must not be oppressed or wronged by king or magistrate or master here.

4. Jesus Christ by the grace of God tasted death for every man.

Thus he became the propitiation for the sins of the world through whom the offer of pardon for offences against God was to be made to every man. This was the most wonderful of all the truths proclaimed by the gospel, and could not fail to exert a mighty influence in awakening the minds of men.

By receiving the offered grace and gift of righteousness any one of the human family would acquire the privileges of a child of God. Though still as a creature subject to vanity in common with all mankind, he had the hope of deliverance at once imparted to him. Henceforth his earnest expectation stood with extended foot and outstretched neck, waiting for the liberty of the sons of God, as a garrison, closely besieged, stand undismayed on their walls watching for the standard of their deliverer gleaming along the mountain heights. Nor could his expectation be put to shame. The manifestation for which he waited would be made, either partly even in this world or completely and gloriously in the world to come.

Thus he was raised in spirit above the power of oppression, and, while patiently enduring wrong, was acquiring strength which rendered the infliction of that wrong hazardous to the oppressor.

5. THE DISCIPLES OF CHRIST MADE THEMSELVES STRONG AMONG MEN BY THEIR READINESS TO LAY DOWN THEIR LIVES IN DEFENCE OF HIS CAUSE.

A striking illustration of the general principle here involved is found in the early history of Rome.

When that city was besieged by Porsenna, king of Etruria, Mucius Scævola resolved to take the invader's life at the risk of his own. Having by mistake killed only a subordinate officer, he at once boldly avowed to the king what his object had been, and assured him that he need not expect to escape, as three hundred young men had, like himself, resolved to risk their lives in taking his. Porsenna was not afraid of all the armies Rome could raise, so long as they were governed by the ordinary principles of human nature; but three hundred young men who had made up their minds to die he did not dare to encounter: consequently, he proposed terms for an immediate peace. So is it everywhere where life is magnanimously risked for the accomplishment of a noble purpose. They who do it, often when many things are against them, make themselves illustrious by success; or, if they fall, they leave behind them an influence which may be felt in distant lands and to the latest times.

Pre-eminently has this been so in the progress of Christianity. When its Founder was lifted up on the cross he secured the gathering of all men unto him; and when his disciples—the high and low, the learned and ignorant, men and women, old men and children—impelled by his precepts and pressing on in his steps, counted not their lives dear to them, shrank not from death when threatened by arbitrary power, and spurned deliverance at the cost of the slightest dishonor to their Saviour's name,—then did the dignity of human nature receive its noblest demonstration at the hands of man. Its rights were vindicated at the moment when most trampled on; when it was weak, then it became strong, and when it sank in death its triumph was achieved.

Sect. 3.—The Effects Produced.

"Have turned the world upside down."

The diffusion of the gospel actually produced the movement among the people which its principles were so well adapted to arouse.

Wherever the Saviour went multitudes crowded around him. His fame spread abroad, awakening, arousing, stimulating the people. Those of them who received not his teaching concerning the life to come were greatly excited with hope as to this life. They desired to take him by force and make him their king. They went forth to meet him, shouting with triumphant acclaim, "Blessed is the King of Israel!"

They who held the people in subjection trembled for their power, and said to each other, "Perceive ye how ye prevail nothing? behold, the world is gone after him." They dreaded a revolution in his behalf that might bring on them a heavier infliction of their Conqueror's power: "If we let him thus alone, all men will believe on him, and the Romans will come and take away both our place and nation."

Their last and apparently successful argument with Pilate was an appeal to the political consequences that might be expected from the release of Jesus: "If thou let this man go thou art not Cæsar's friend; he that maketh himself a king speaketh against Cæsar."

After the ascension of Jesus, when his disciples proclaimed the gospel, the multitude were excited with intense emotion. Jerusalem was filled with the doctrine. The councilors of Israel were in great perplexity, unable to foresee what would be the result of the movement, at a loss what to do in order to arrest it, and afraid to use violence lest the people should rise in their strength against them.

When the heralds of the gospel were driven out of Jerusalem they went everywhere proclaiming it, and everywhere it produced the same stirring up of the people. They who received it hailed it with joy; they who rejected it opposed it violently; both kinds of treatment were counterparts of the popular movement it produced.

Mental activity was stimulated by the assemblage of the people to hear the new doctrine; by the miracles that were wrought openly to attest it; by daily examination of the written evidence adduced for it; by public discussions and judicial trials.

Sometimes the people with one accord gave heed; often they were divided in opinion; on several occasions they made an assault on the speakers. At one place opposition was excited by grave men and honorable women; at another, wretches of the baser sort gathered a mob and set the town in an uproar. In one city, craftsmen, alarmed for the profits of their trade, assembled riotously together; in another, national prejudice, indignant at the intrusion of foreigners and furious at the progress of the new system, burst into a tempest before which even a Roman guard gave way.

The proclaimers of the gospel were accused of troubling cities, of fomenting treason and of turning the world upside down. They were brought before magistrates of all grades, and stood even at the imperial throne. Some of these officers wisely resolved to let them alone; others drove their accusers from the tribunal; a third class courted bribes from the one party and popularity from the other. Some treated the prisoners kindly; others threatened them, beat them, shut them up in prison, and put them to death.

In no place did the gospel fail to stir up popular activity. Starting from the meanest town of Galilee, it became powerful by the number of its adherents in the most splendid cities of Asia. Entering .Europe at the outskirts of Philippi, and being first spoken there only to women, it startled the Greeks as the trumpet blast of their own criers; called into exercise their logic, their wisdom, their curiosity; forced the Epicurean and the Stoic into strange alliance, and crowded Mars' Hill with a brilliant array of excited intellect around one whom they stigmatized as a barbarian and a babbler. At Rome the numbers of converts rapidly increased, chiefly among the humbler classes, but including some also of high rank. They soon attracted the notice of the government at home, and were spoken of in the most distant cities as believers in the new religion.

Throughout the empire similar results were witnessed. In cities, towns, villages and rural districts great numbers of Christians were found. Tacitus, whose concise phrase must be assigned its utmost force, says there was "a vast multitude" of them. Tertullian, the wings of whose flight always need clipping, declares that "if the numerous host of Christians had retired from the empire into some remote region, the loss of so many men would have left a hideous gap and inflicted a shameful scar on the government. It would have stood aghast at its desolation and been struck dumb at the silence and horror of nature, as if the whole world had departed."

This multitude were linked together as one people. They spake of themselves as "We" and were described by others as "They;" "the Christians;" "the Nazarenes;" "the Atheists." They were united by a common religion, common sufferings, joys and hopes. In exile, on missionary tours and commercial journeys, strangers from distant regions were received as friends. Assailed by adversaries all around them, they pressed more and more closely together. Hated by their enemies, it was said of them more earnestly: "Behold how they love one another." In the fervor of affection even hostile nationalities were melted down, and there remained neither Greek nor Jew, barbarian, Scythian, bond nor free. Thus they became a people in the midst of an empire.

Scattered abroad everywhere, they pressed with unremitting force against the imperial authority. In matters purely civil, their religion directed them to obey the emperor: "Ye must needs be subject not only for wrath, but also for conscience' sake." But the pagan religion (as we have said) was so identified with the state that it was impossible to renounce the one without often disobeying the other. In domestic arrangements, in social intercourse, in amusements, in daily labor, in the camp, the forum and the senate, the national religion, clothed with the authority of law, asserted its jurisdiction. Consequently, Christians were compelled often to disobey the laws in proportion as they obeyed their conscience and God. From the refusal to adorn their doors with evergreens to the denial of divine honors to the emperor, their action with respect to religion was a continued course of rebellion. And as rebellion against any law, however unimportant in itself, is an attack against the sovereign authority, if not subdued it weakens that authority and has a tendency to overthrow it. A rebellion that acquired so many adherents, that extended to all matters of religion, and that no lenity could allure or rage subdue, must at last have effected the destruction of the empire which had exerted all its power in vain to destroy it.

But an unlooked-for event arrested the process and postponed the result. The emperor Constantine, either truly converted to Christianity or adopting it as a master-stroke of policy, proclaimed it as the national religion. Thus the rebellion, without any change in itself, suddenly became loyalty, and the whole measure of obedience to God gave for a time its support to the shaken empire of man.

Long ago, it is said in an old legend, the dead body of a noble lady was buried, and a tomb of solid masonry erected over it. But living seed had somehow been lodged in the soil, from which seven trees sprang up, making their way through the crevices of the tomb, and by their constantly expanding energy forcing apart the cement, clamps and blocks of marble, until the whole was shaken; then with their branches they embraced the fragments, bound them together and prevented for a time their fall. So when freedom was buried at Rome, and the emperors were rearing the massive structure of despotism over the grave, the good seed of the kingdom of heaven had been widely diffused. From it sprang trees of religious liberty, not seven in number or seventy times seven, but innumerable. They insinuated themselves into every aperture, and, growing with irrepressible energy, forced asunder cement and clamps and marble, until the vast fabric tottered in every part; then their wide-spread branches, intertwining themselves among the fragments, bound them together and delayed their fall.

CHAPTER II.

THE REPUBLICS ORGANIZED.

"He separated the disciples."

THE religious liberty which Christianity awakened among its disciples it organized into republics.

Here we assert that the primitive Christian churches were republics, and proceed to establish the proposition by showing the republican qualities—

I. Of the churches.

II. Of their officers.

Sect. 1.—The Republican Qualities of the Churches.

"Two or three in my name."

I. *Their constitution was republican.*

Every company of professed believers in Christ was a church. They derived their right to associate themselves together from their individual rights as believers, expressly sanctioned by Him whose authority they owned: "WHERE TWO OR THREE ARE GATHERED TOGETHER IN MY NAME, THERE AM I IN THE MIDST OF THEM."

This is a full and sufficient charter for all who comply with its terms. It recognizes the right of associating together as belonging to *two believers*—the smallest number that can possibly exercise it. It defines the character of the association, "in the name of Christ," as distinguished from every other that can be formed in the world. It guarantees to it his presence—the highest privilege that can be conferred on men. It binds them in subjection to his laws prescribed for the government of his Church.

Every such association is a church of Christ before its officers are appointed, giving existence to them, not deriving existence from them, as a tree has existence before its branches, especially before the loftiest of them. If they boast, yet they bear not the root, but the root bears them.

A strong support of this position is supplied by the apostolic epistles. These are all addressed *to the churches,* while officers are either not referred to at all or only as having their place in the church. The epistle which stands first in the common arrangement of the New Testament was written to the church in the imperial city, whose officers, as the inspired writer well knew, would at length claim supreme authority over their own church and all others throughout the world. Surely, if this stupendous claim had been genuine, here would have been an appropriate place to recognize it; here at least we might suppose a germ of it would have been planted, to be developed in due time. Yet this epistle is addressed "to all in Rome who were beloved of God and called to be saints." So far from ascribing lordly superiority to the officers of the church, or from saying anything that could help to develop it, it contains not the slighest allusion to officers at all, until toward the close, in the exhortations "to every man," they come to view in their place. And of those exhortations the first, the keynote of the rest, is that "no man should cherish lofty thoughts or arrogate to himself more than had been given him."[1] Is there not evidence here that the inspired writer, instead of laying down laws for a spiritual empire to be lorded over by a vicegerent of Christ, was wisely guarding the equality of a republican church?

This evidence the subsequent epistles all strengthen. They are addressed "to the church of God which is at Corinth;" "to the churches of Galatia;" "to the saints at Ephesus;" "to all in Christ Jesus at Philippi, *with the officers*;" "to the

[1] Rom. xii. 3.

saints and faithful brethren at Colosse;" "to the church of the Thessalonians;" "to the holy brethren, partakers of the heavenly calling;" "to the twelve tribes;" "to the strangers scattered through Asia Minor who had obtained precious faith;" "to Christians generally," and "to the seven churches of Asia," with a special message "to the angel of each church."

Therefore, both from the charter granted by the Saviour and from the instructions sent in his name, we conclude that his churches were republics, in which all the members were equally subject to him, and had equal rights among themselves.

II. *The republican character of the primitive churches is shown by the fact that they elected their own officers.*

1. Election of an apostle.

The very first act performed by the church after the ascension of Christ was the election of an apostle in the place of Judas.

If the Saviour, after his resurrection, had filled the vacancy by his own act, the new apostle would have manifestly stood on equal ground with the eleven. To some minds it may appear strange that he did not adopt this plan, yet the fact that he did not is clear.

He might have directed the apostles to make the choice in his name, or, without special direction, they might have considered themselves authorized to make it. If they had done so, the validity of their action would probably not have been questioned by the church. Certainly such an exercise of authority would have agreed very well with much that has been said concerning their governing power. But the fact concerning them also is clear that they did not, by their separate action as apostles, fill the vacancy in their own ranks. Indeed, it is remarkable that they do not appear in the narrative as a separate class, except so far as Peter, being one of them, may be supposed to have spoken in their name, and as the person chosen was received among them.

Peter stood up in the midst of the whole church, which then contained about one hundred and twenty members, telling them what it was necessary for them to do and what were the qualifications requisite for the office.

In response to his address the whole church, the company among whom he was standing, proceeded to act. Their action consisted of several particulars:

(1.) *The nomination of candidates for the office.*

"They appointed two, Joseph and Matthias."[1] They set them forth as eligible to the office according to the qualifications that had been declared.

"It was not the apostles," as a separate class, who made the nomination, "but the whole assembly whom Peter had addressed. It is clear that the membership were held to be on an equal footing."[2]

This nomination by them was an essential and primary part of the election. It practically restricted the final choice to one of these two.

(2.) *Their prayer to Christ that he would show them which of the two he preferred.*

"The same entire body of members present proceeded to pray."[3]

This also was part of the process adopted and carried into effect by the choice and consent of the whole church.

(3.) "*They gave their lots.*"[4]

Many conclude from these words that Matthias was chosen "*by lot*" according to the practice common among the Jews. On the other hand, reasons are not wanting in support of the opinion that the meaning of this phrase really is, "*They gave their votes.*"

[1] Acts i. 23. [2] Jacobus in loc. [3] Ibid.

[4] Acts i. 26.

The determining of the question is not essential to the establishment of the proposition before us, that the election was the act of the whole church. For if the more common interpretation be correct, that the lot was used, then *it was the whole church* who adopted and practiced that method of appealing to Christ and of deciding the question between the two candidates. *They gave their lots.* Their agreement to do so must have been reached by their votes, either formally or informally given. Whatever of human action was put forth was the action of the whole church. This view of the case is well expressed by Dr. Jacobus. "It was necessary always that an apostle should be chosen by the Lord himself. Hence they adopted the lot. Yet the body of the disciples had also a part to take and a voice in the election. Hence the distinct mention is made of the whole number of disciples present, to signify thus their equality as called on to express their choice as far as it could go."

(4.) *After the choice had fallen on Matthias, whether by a majority of votes or by lot, "he was numbered with the eleven apostles."*

The original word,[1] translated "was numbered," is derived from "ψηφος," which without dispute

[1] συγκατεψηφισθη.

means *a vote.* It denotes a decision made by the votes of a court or of a popular assembly. As here employed it probably means that after the choice had devolved on Matthias, the whole assembly ratified it either by their unanimous vote, formally given, or by their cordial consent to his being numbered among the apostles.[1]

All these particulars combined together—their nomination of the candidates, their prayer to be shown which of the two Christ preferred, their voting or casting their lots and their final concurrence in the choice of Matthias—clearly amount to an election by the church.

Let us here mark the significance of the act we record. Surrounded with a despotism that had been established by military power and that grasped at dominion over all human affairs, this company of a hundred men, in a retired room, placed one of their own number in office over themselves. That first act of Christian freemen, unconscious as they were of its far-reaching tendencies, was the beginning of a practice which was to be extended among all mankind, and to transform the governments of the world.

[1] In the translation made at Geneva, 1557, the rendering is, "Was by a common consent counted with."—*Eng. Hexapla.*

2. Election of deacons.

On the day of Pentecost and soon after, many thousands of persons were added to the Christian community. Of these a large proportion were strangers from distant places, who had come to Jerusalem to attend the annual feasts. Not expecting to remain long, many of them had brought only limited means of support. Consequently, when their conversion to Christianity impelled them to prolong their stay, provision for their wants had to be made by the brethren who were at home in the city or who had resources at command. Large sums for this purpose were at once spontaneously offered, which (as no one had any special authority to receive and manage them) were naturally entrusted to the apostles' care.

But they soon felt the necessity of relieving themselves from the charge, not only that they might be free to attend to their peculiar duties, but probably also because they foresaw that evils would arise if the funds of the church were held by the same officers who exercised spiritual authority. They therefore at once adopted a plan to meet the emergency. Calling together "*the multitude of the disciples*," they proposed to them that they should "*select for themselves*" seven men of suitable qualifications to take charge of the pecuniary affairs.

The proposition "*pleased the whole multitude,*" and they accordingly elected—"*chose out for themselves*"—the seven men, who were installed into office by the laying on of the apostles' hands.

3. ELECTION TO OFFICE THE GENERAL PRACTICE.

Thus, at the very beginning of Christianity, an apostle and seven very important officers were elected by the universal suffrage of the church. These elections, held at the instance of the apostles, we are warranted to suppose, would be regarded as precedents and would be generally followed. It remains to inquire whether in fact elections to office by the people were general among the primitive churches.

We have already shown that the epistles were addressed *to the churches* as under God the source of action and government. It is fair to conclude that the choice of their own officers—a privilege resting on the foundation-stone of sovereignty, and not attended with greater difficulty than others clearly exercised by them—would certainly be secured to them.

Nor is there, so far as we know, in the New

Testament, any positive or even probable declaration that the apostles appointed church officers irrespective of the choice of the people. Paul and Barnabas, we are told in our translation, *ordained elders* in every church during their journey through Asia Minor. The exact meaning of the original phrase[1] is made obscure by its conciseness, only a single word being employed to include the whole process of choice and appointment. It signifies literally "to stretch forth the hand," and was clearly used among the Greeks to denote *elections in popular assemblies by show of hands.* It occurs only one other time in the New Testament, and then evidently denotes election by the church.[2] In the instance before us[3] we are told that Paul and Barnabas performed the action denoted by the word. It is this fact which causes the difficulty in determining what that action was. But, if we suppose that the verb is used in a *causative sense*—a sense which often occurs in classic as well as Hebraistic Greek —then the meaning is that Paul and Barnabas

[1] Χειροτονησαντες.

[2] 2 Cor. viii. 19: "Was chosen of the churches." In the Geneva translation we find "Chosen by the election of the churches."—*Eng. Hexapla.*

[3] Acts xiv. 23.

caused an election of elders to be made in every church.

This is just what other facts and analogies would lead us to conclude that they did. They took care that elders were elected—probably they presided at the meeting of the church when the election was held.

If this be the true force of the word, the passage must be added to the evidence already considered that each church elected its officers.

But if this interpretation be rejected, the only other that retains the idea of *stretching forth the hand* is that which makes it equivalent to the imposition of hands. The sense would then be that the apostle and his companion ordained the elders by the laying on of hands. This is the meaning the word actually acquired in the subsequent history of the church. It is also evidently the one adopted by our translators. If it be correct, Paul's own practice must be classed with his direction to Timothy "to commit the truth to faithful men," and to Titus, "to ordain elders." All these terms will then alike describe installation into office. But that is distinct from election to office. In our own country a diocesan bishop institutes a rector, a presbytery installs a pastor, and a judge inaugurates a governor or president, all of whom have been previously elected by the people. Without the election the installation could not take place. Therefore the fact that apostles, their associates and deputies ordained church officers is no proof that these had not been previously elected by the church. The inference rather is that they had been, and it is confirmed by the identity of the word employed in the direction to Titus, *καταστησης*, with that used by the apostles when they offered to install into office the deacons who should be elected by the church.

Its appropriate force is "to establish in office;" and since the act of the apostles in the case of the deacons was after the choice by the church, there is nothing to diminish the previous probability that the similar act of Titus in the case of elders was to follow a similar choice.

While there are no accounts of appointment to office inconsistent with a previous election by the church, there are repeated records of officers having been elected for the performance of specific duties. Some of these were the messengers of the churches to convey their contributions to distant brethren. Of one—to whose case we have just referred—it is expressly added not only that his praise was in the churches, but also that he had been *elected by the churches* to the work.[1]

When the church at Jerusalem heard of the spread of the truth *they sent forth* Barnabas to aid in its advance. When the discussion arose at Antioch with the Judaizing teachers, *the church determined to send* delegates to Jerusalem concerning it. In reply, *the apostles and elders, with the whole church, sent chosen men* to Antioch. When in the Corinthian church there arose a division with reference to Apollos, Paul recognized their right to have him as their chosen minister, for he wrote to them concerning him, "I greatly desired him to come unto you, but his will was not at all to come now."

All these are not only instances of election by the church to particular offices, but also manifest parts of a system in which election to office was the common practice.

4. Passing to uninspired history, we find that churches near the apostolic age elected their pastors. Clement, one of the earliest pastors of the church at Rome, was chosen by the unanimous voice of the church.[2] He also declares that officers were ordained—using the same word as that which designates the installation of deacons and elders—

[1] 2 Cor. viii. 19. [2] Bower's Hist. of Popes, vol. i., p. 7.

at first by the apostles and afterward by other approved men, "*the whole church having given their consent.*"[1]

This was plainly the extension of the practice of election by the church as recorded in the New Testament.

Satisfied, therefore, that the republican character of the primitive churches is shown by their election of their own officers, we here arrest our examination of the topic, adding only that, as we recede from apostolic times, we shall find one restriction after another placed on elections, until they are at length wrested entirely from the people. This fact will furnish additional proof that elections by the people were introduced at the very beginning of Christianity, seeing that they could not have been introduced at any subsequent time.

Sect. 2.—The Republican Qualities of the Officers.

"*Elders in every church.*"

1. *There was a plurality of officers in each church.*

In our inquiry concerning the officers of particular churches we do not include the apostles, whose mission extended over the field of the world. Some of them, we know, continued a long time at

[1] Neander, vol. i., p. 189.

Jerusalem, but in addition to them the church there had, from the beginning, its own elders. At Antioch there were prophets and teachers. In the churches that Paul and Barnabas organized there were ordained elders. The church at Ephesus had its elders or bishops, and that of Philippi its bishops and deacons. Timothy and Titus ordained elders in every city where they established churches.

The Apostle James in his general Epistle takes for granted that wherever there was a church there were elders. Peter also exhorts the elders who had charge of the flock of God through all the provinces of Asia Minor.

These instances are enough to show that every primitive church had a plurality of officers.

2. *Among these officers there was equality of rank.*

When Paul sent for the elders of the church at Ephesus, he addressed them together, as being equals in rank, exercising the same office and subject to the same responsibility. They had a joint guardianship over the church, and were consequently directed to take heed to all the flock over which the Holy Spirit had made them overseers, to feed the church of God.

The deacons were not subordinate to the elders. They had different duties assigned them, and are not to be compared as to rank with the elders, either as being higher or lower. Both offices required men of exalted and tried character. The original seven were distinguished for integrity and were full of the Holy Ghost and wisdom. And, by comparing the qualifications specified in the directions to Timothy, we find that always the deacons were to be of equal standing with the elders, except that teaching formed no part of their official duty.

The practice, therefore, of subordinating the deacons to the elders and of regarding them both as two grades of a threefold order of ministers was unknown in the primitive churches.

While there was equality of rank among the officers of churches, we may take for granted that in general, if not always, they chose one of their number to preside over them. Experience clearly shows that to promote order and efficiency among equals a presiding officer is indispensable. The choice may be made at every meeting, for a stated period, or for an indefinite time. Nor does the appointment of such an officer alter the republican character of the organization. In our own country every public meeting has its chairman; every municipal council, legislative body and commonwealth its presiding officer; every Presbyterian church session, presbytery and assembly its moderator. None of these are, on that account, any less republican.

We have now shown from the New Testament that, in the plurality and equality of their chosen officers, as well as by their constitution, the primitive Christian churches were republics.

Sect. 3.—Unity among the Churches.

"*That they all may be one.*"

While, however, these republics were complete, each in its own sphere, they were not isolated from each other, but were all one in Christ their Head. Life in all its grades is endowed by its divine Author with organizing power. At the beginning, when the Spirit of God brooded over the elements of matter, they began to attract each other and combine together. The same power that formed of them a single world and placed it in its own orbit connected it also with a system of worlds of similar organization, and these again with other systems extending, beyond the ability of man to find a limit, toward infinitude of space. Vegetable life, existing in a germ, organizes into one tree the massive trunk, the giant branches, the myriad leaves, and, having its seed in itself, spreads abroad after its kind from year to year, from land to land. Human life organizes its many members into one body, and is expanded by one blood, from one generation to another, into all the nations of men on all the face of the earth.

So spiritual life in Christ, existing in the hearts of believers with an organizing power limited only by "the measure of the gift of Christ," forms into one church not two or three only, but large numbers in a community, and multitudes in the same land, in different nations, from age to age, to the ends of the earth and in heavenly worlds. "For, as the body is one, and hath many members, and all the members of that one body, being many, are one body, so also is Christ. For by one spirit are we all baptized into one body, whether Jews or Gentiles, whether bond or free;[1] till we all come in the unity of the faith, and of the knowledge of the Son of God, unto a perfect man, unto the measure of the stature of the fullness of Christ, from whom the whole body fitly joined together and compacted by that which every joint supplieth, according to the effectual working in the measure of every part, maketh increase of the body unto the building up of itself in love."[2]

[1] 1 Cor. xii. 12, 13. [2] Eph. iv. 13, 16.

CHAPTER III.

THE REPUBLICS TRANSFORMED.

"Another wild beast (θηριον), coming up out of the earth, exerciseth all the power of the first wild beast that was before his eyes."

THE second division of the work of establishing republican government in the world met with a partial and temporary failure, similar in some respects to that which had attended the first.

As, in the first, the Hebrew commonwealth had been displaced by a royal government like those of other lands, so, in the second, the republican Christian churches were transformed into a monarchy by assimilation to the imperial power. In the first, however, the monarchies imitated were outside of the Jewish nation; in the second, the churches were within the empire; in the one, the destruction of the republic was willful and instantaneous; in the other, the transformation into a monarchy was by a gradual process, scarcely suspected, at first, even by those who took part in carrying it on.

This gradual process comprised a triple change:

I. The rise of monarchy in the churches.

II. The addition of temporal power to spiritual rule.

III. The wresting away of elections to office out of the hands of the people.

Sect. 1.—Monarchy Rising in the Churches.

"Who exalteth himself."

We have shown that by the diffusion of Christianity republican churches were established in the midst of a despotic civil government.

These Christ designed should extend everywhere and be faithfully maintained. The contrariety between them and the civil government he had deliberately chosen and solemnly ordained: "*Ye know that they who are accounted to rule over the Gentiles exercise lordship over them, and their great ones exercise authority over them.* BUT SO SHALL IT NOT BE AMONG YOU; *but whosoever will be great among you shall be your minister, and whosoever of you will be the chiefest shall be the servant of all.*"[1]

Had this contrariety, so positively commanded, been maintained by the republican churches, the imperial government would have been transformed. It was greatly affected, as we have shown in a pre-

[1] Mark x. 42–44.

vious chapter,[1] and its continuance endangered, by the vital energy with which the principles of Christianity were at first diffused. But instead of intelligently and resolutely adhering to the direction, "So SHALL IT NOT BE AMONG YOU," the officers of churches gradually imitated the "lordship and authority" which were exercised around them, and to which, in all matters except those of religion, they and their brethren were accustomed to yield.

Situated as they were, it was difficult for them to avoid the imitation entirely, and when they fell into it the people would not notice it or be alarmed at its progress. Their whole lives were moving on under royal authority, and if in the midst of them another similar force should begin and increase, it would at first exert no perceptible influence on their condition, nor would they have any conception of what its ultimate strength and results would be.

The imitation took place both in the spirit and manner of executing the republican offices, and in the actual elevation of one man over the other officers and over the church. At first, as we have seen, a plurality of bishops existed in each church. To one of these at an early period, perhaps from

[1] Part II., chap. i.

the beginning, the office of president was assigned. This may have been done either informally, by a tacit yielding to the oldest or the most gifted presbyter, or by a regular election. But, in whatever way he obtained the office, the president at first neither claimed nor possessed any superiority of rank over his colleagues. His actions were performed in their name and with their assent. There was, however, in his breast that love of authority which is natural to men. There was also near at hand a civil officer who, having been clothed with authority by the emperor, was exercising "lordship" over the people. The president, the other bishops and the whole church had always before them the robes, the insignia and the power of this imperial functionary. All their ideas were formed and cherished in the atmosphere of official authority. Their whole lives were controlled by official power.

Amidst such influences a change imperceptibly took place in the church. We need not suppose that it always began with the presiding officer. The other presbyters were as likely to promote it as he. The idea that they were separated from the people as an "order," and were elevated over them as rulers, would spring up in their minds simultaneously with the notions which he was beginning to cherish of authority over *them*. The growth in their own pretensions would incline them to promote the similar growth in his. They would be as ready to yield authority as he would be to claim it. Perhaps they pressed on him assumptions which he had as yet no disposition to attempt.

We may here mark off some of the principal stages in the ascent from the plain of republican equality to the summit of monarchical rule.

I. The growth of a monarchical spirit.

The change would be manifested at first in the tone and manner of the officer in executing his undoubted duties.

His actions in the name of his colleagues and of his church would gradually be performed in his own. That which they yielded unconsciously, or as a favor, or on a special occasion, he would retain as a prerogative conferred from heaven. That which began by permission of the church was transformed in its progress to authority over the church.

That such a change was likely to occur might be inferred from the warning of Christ: "Whosoever will be great among you, let him be your minister, and whosoever will be chief among you, let him be your servant; even as the Son of man came not to be ministered unto, but to minister."

That the process commenced even in the time of the apostles is evident from their writings. When Paul predicted the career of the "man of sin," whose iniquities would be accomplished by EXALTING HIMSELF, he testified that "the mystery was already at work."[1] The last of the apostles says, in his epistle to Gaius, "I wrote unto the church, but Diotrephes, *who loveth to have the preeminence among them*, receiveth us not, . . . prating against us with malicious words; and not content therewith, neither doth he himself receive the brethren, and forbiddeth them that would, and casteth them out of the church."[2] This describes a very considerable advance toward monarchy. If the succession of popes does not date from Diotrephes, he ought to stand early on the list. He claimed the prerogative of rejecting at his pleasure members and officers of churches, and even the most venerable of the apostles, of putting offenders under interdict, and of pronouncing excommunication. These were elements of monarchical power. The principal drawback to them was that lions, crosses and tortures could not be em-

[1] 2 Thess. ii. 3–8. [2] 3 John 9, 10.

ployed, as they were still in the hands of the government officer over the way.

The New Testament also exhibits the actual growth of monarchical power in a single church during a definite period. When Paul, about the year 60, wished to give his parting counsel to the church at Ephesus, he sent for its *bishops* as its official representatives. When the Saviour, about the close of the first century, sent his final message to the same church, he addressed *one man* as if he were then its representative. The difference seems to imply that during forty years a change had been progressing in the Ephesian church. The equality of its officers had been yielding to the rise of one man in influence and power.[1]

The causes which produced this change in one place existed everywhere. There was no such thing at that time as a republican civil government. All power was royal and despotic. Consequently, what was imitated in one place would be in another. The universality of the change would also be promoted by the example and influence of the churches established in large and important cities. There the power of the civil government would be exercised more definitely and with greater

[1] Acts xx. 17, 28; Rev. ii. 1.

splendor. Consequently, the tendency to imitation would be greater, and the churches in their turn would be centres of influence to less important places around them. Thus the original constitution, by which *bishops* had been chosen in every church, gradually verged toward the secondary state expressed by the famous maxim, "No church without *a bishop*."

The jurisdiction of each bishop, as he rose to prelacy, continued to be over a single church.

This is proved by the *number* of bishops. In Asia Minor, a tract of land not much larger than Great Britain, there were about four hundred.[1] At a conference between Augustine and the Donatists, about the year 410, there were present between five and six hundred, from, as it would seem, a single province.[2] From that part of Africa in which the Vandalic persecution raged six hundred and sixty fled, a great number were murdered or imprisoned and many more remained in safety. The whole number in that region, according to this statement, could not have been less than a thousand.[3] What could all these have been but bishops each over a single church?

[1] Bingham. [2] Bishop Burnett.

[3] Victor Uticensis, Fifth Century.

II. THE SECOND STAGE OF THE ASCENT WAS THE EXALTATION OF BISHOPS ACCORDING TO THE POLITICAL RANK OF THE CITIES IN WHICH THEY LIVED.

The episcopal office, held by so many, was at first regarded as possessing essentially equal authority and honor. But by the change wrought in imitation of the civil authority this equality was gradually yet completely destroyed. A series of gradations was established, by which the rank and jurisdiction of a bishop became exactly proportioned to the rank which the city or town or district, in which his church was situated, enjoyed in the empire. Bishops in the country came to be accounted inferior to those in towns; those in unimportant towns to those in more splendid cities. And as among the latter a few were very conspicuous in position and wealth, the rank of their civil rulers was the standard to which the dignity of their bishops approached. Over all, prior to the accession of Constantine, three cities, ANTIOCH, ALEXANDRIA and ROME, enjoyed unquestioned superiority, the former two as having been the seats of splendid monarchies; the latter, as the capital of the empire. *In accordance with this superiority, we find the bishops of these three cities gradually rising in rank above all others.*

But these cities were not equal among themselves in civil rank. Antioch had depended for her grandeur mainly on being a royal city. Consequently, after the Syrian monarchy was overthrown, it gradually decayed, and ranked as the *third* city of the empire. After the conquest of Egypt the importance of Alexandria was sustained by commerce. Hence it was accounted the second city. And as Rome was "the great city, which reigned over all," none disputed the first place with her. *In precise proportion to this scale of secular grandeur was the rank of the bishops, yielded at first imperceptibly by custom, and determined at a later period by the votes of councils.* THE BISHOP OF ANTIOCH WAS ASSIGNED THE THIRD POSITION, THE BISHOP OF ALEXANDRIA THE SECOND AND THE BISHOP OF ROME THE FIRST.

III. THESE GRADATIONS IN RANK WERE FORMALLY ESTABLISHED BY THE WILL OF THE EMPEROR.

The changes which we have thus far described were in progress during the first three centuries. The imitation of the civil government by the churches was, however, necessarily imperfect so long as Christianity continued a religion unrecognized by the state. But when the Emperor Constantine became a professed Christian there was a rapid maturing of the change. The authority that had been creeping on slowly in the footsteps of custom was now suddenly proclaimed with the majesty of law.

The presence of the emperor as a new power in the affairs of the churches was signally manifested by the council of Nice, convened by him at the suggestion of some of the bishops in the year 325. "The formal opening of the council was made by his stately entrance, which Eusebius thus describes: 'After all the bishops had entered the central building of the royal palace, each silently awaited the arrival of the emperor. The moment his approach was announced they all rose from their seats, and the emperor appeared, like a heavenly messenger of God, covered with gold and gems—a glorious presence, very tall and full of beauty, strength and majesty. When he reached the golden throne prepared for him he stopped and sat not down until the bishops gave him the sign. And after him they all resumed their seats.'

"How great the contrast between this position of the church and the time of her persecution but scarcely passed! What a revolution of opinion in bishops, who had once feared the Roman emperor as their worst enemy, and who now greeted him in his half-barbarous attire as an angel of God from heaven, and gave him, though not yet baptized, the honorary presidency of the highest assembly of the church!"[1]

The place which he thus assumed in the church virtually identified the civil and ecclesiastical governments. He who exercised lordship absolutely over the nations henceforth exercised it also in growing measure over the churches. Thus the command of Christ, "*So shall it not be among you,*" was reversed, and the transformation of the churches from independent associated republics to a consolidated department of the empire was advanced.

The emperor having become practically the head of the church, under his influence the hierarchy was definitely established in close imitation of the various grades among the civil rulers. The empire was divided, as to its secular government, into four prefectures; these were subdivided into dioceses, and the dioceses into provinces. The rulers of cities and districts were subject to the governor of their province; the governors of provinces to the governor of their diocese; the gov-

[1] Dr. Schaff in "Hours at Home."

ernors of dioceses to their prefect, and the prefects to the emperor.

In like manner the bishops of cities and districts were subjected to the metropolitan of their province; the metropolitans of the provinces to the metropolitan of their diocese; the metropolitans of the dioceses to the patriarchs of one of the four cities, Rome, Antioch, Alexandria and Constantinople, and the patriarchs of these cities, like the prefects, had no superior except the emperor.

IV. THE BISHOPS OF THE TWO IMPERIAL CITIES WERE EXALTED ABOVE ALL OTHERS.

As the imperial grandeur of Constantinople increased, the importance of Antioch and Alexandria decayed, leaving the new capital without rival, the first city of the East.

In equal degree, the bishop thereof, thinking the see raised with the city, taking great state on himself, began to act as if he were as much exalted above other bishops as his city was above other cities. This gave great offence to his brethren; yet as his paramount interest at court enabled him to oblige or disoblige whom he pleased, they chose rather to gain his favor by yielding to his ambition than to incur his displeasure by opposing it. In the year 383 the bishop of the capital was already so far exalted by the connivance and tacit consent of his colleagues as to take precedence of all the bishops of the East. Hence at the council held that year the bishop of Constantinople was called to preside, in neglect of the patriarch of Alexandria, who had hitherto been acknowledged as first in dignity after the bishop of Rome. By this act the council declared that, agreeably to the established custom (that bishops should rank according to the rank of their cities), *the bishop of new Rome should have the first place of honor after that of* OLD ROME.[1]

By this canon no positive jurisdiction was added to the first bishop of the East. He was only placed in rank and dignity next to the bishop of Rome.

But, having secured the title, he began to exercise gradually a corresponding degree of power. Beginning with Thrace, and alleging that Constantinople, which was the head of that diocese according to the civil polity, ought to be so according to the ecclesiastical, which was founded on the civil, he assumed at once the title, claimed the rights and exercised, within the limits of the diocese, all the jurisdiction peculiar to a patriarch. In the next place, he succeeded in obtaining the same jurisdiction in

[1] Bower's Hist. of Popes, vol. i., p. 215.

the dioceses of Pontus and Asia, and afterward in the patriarchate of Antioch. Thus, in the course of a few years, of the five dioceses into which the East was divided four were subjected to the see of Constantinople.

Application was then made to the council of Chalcedon, in the year 451, to confirm the authority which had been assumed. By that council the decree was re-enacted which placed the bishop of new Rome next in dignity to that of old Rome; a patriarchal jurisdiction was vested in him over the dioceses of Pontus, Asia and Thrace; and, in general, all the rights, prerogatives and privileges were granted to him that had been enjoyed by the bishop of Rome. For doing so they assigned this reason: "Whereas the see of Old Rome had been, not undeservedly, distinguished by the fathers with some privileges *because that city was the seat of empire,* the fathers of Constantinople were prompted by the same motive to distinguish the most holy see of new Rome with equal privileges, thinking it fit that the city which they saw honored with the empire and the senate, and equaled in every civil privilege to old Rome, should be likewise equaled to her in ecclesiastical matters."[1]

[1] Bower, vol. i., p. 221. Neander, vol. ii., p. 164.

THUS AS THERE WERE NOW TWO IMPERIAL CITIES EXALTED ABOVE ALL OTHERS, SO THE BISHOPS OF THESE TWO CITIES WERE EXALTED ABOVE THOSE OF ALL OTHERS.

V. THE CONTEST FOR SUPREMACY BETWEEN THE BISHOPS OF CONSTANTINOPLE AND ROME.

The process of exaltation had not yet reached its height. Other rivalship having been distanced, Constantinople was now the great rival of Rome.

Hitherto the latter had been first in honor and power. She still enjoyed the prestige which the greatness of a thousand years had given her, and which the upstart magnificence of the new city could not at once take away. But the tide was ebbing from the Tiber to the Bosphorus. The presence, wealth and majesty of the emperor had been removed from the one to the other. Hence, as the new city was adorned and favored, the old insensibly declined. In the rivalship between them, the Western capital depended on the past; the Eastern was elated with the triumph of the present. In such a contest the victory, though it might be delayed, was sure. Rome at length sank beneath the superiority of Constantinople.

In like manner the supremacy of the Western prelate bowed before that of the Eastern, to whom, in the year 595, the title of UNIVERSAL BISHOP was given by the emperor, and was confirmed by the assembly of patriarchs, metropolitans and senators. Gregory the Great, who was at that time bishop of Rome, filled with jealousy by this exaltation of his rival over himself, denounced the new title as execrable, blasphemous and infernal, and applied to him who should assume it the address of Isaiah to Lucifer: "Thou hast said in thine heart, 'I will ascend into heaven, I will exalt my throne above the stars of God; I will be like the Most High.'" But notwithstanding his anathemas the title was retained.

In this extremity succor from an unexpected source was at hand for the bishop of Rome. Phocas, a centurion, described by historians as deformed in person and savage in mind, was raised to the throne by insurgent soldiers, and to secure himself thereon murdered the emperor and his sons in cold blood. This monster the bishop of Rome hastened to acknowledge, ascribing his accession to the special providence of God, and calling on angels in heaven and men on earth to render him glory and praise.

In return for this precious benediction, and for similar support received from Boniface, the successor of Gregory, the usurper in the year 607 took away the envied title from the bishop of Constantinople and conferred it on the bishop of Rome.[1]

VI. THE BISHOP OF ROME BECOMES SOLE RULER OF THE WESTERN CHURCH, AND CLAIMS, AS VICEGERENT OF CHRIST, JURISDICTION OVER ALL THE WORLD.

As might have been expected, the Eastern bishop would not renounce the pre-eminence that had been conferred on him. Therefore with equal titles both renewed their contests for supremacy.

At length, in the ninth century, a furious storm arose between the rival sees, which swept over Christendom, and, though sometimes lulled, continued to rage through several centuries, and finally tore asunder the Western and the Eastern churches.

With the decline of the empire the grandeur of the Eastern church was obscured until, in the fifteenth century, both church and empire disappeared from the field of history, overwhelmed by the Ottoman power and the Mohammedan faith.

On the other hand, with the rise of new kingdoms and the conversion of new nations in the West, the pope of Rome was lifted up higher and higher as the head of the universal church, and, as

[1] Bower, vol. i., p. 426.

the vicegerent of Christ, swaying the sceptre of spiritual monarchy over all the world. Transcending even Lucifer's presumptuous flight, he fulfilled the most awful words ever written of a creature by a prophet's pen: "WHO EXALTETH HIMSELF ABOVE ALL THAT IS CALLED GOD OR THAT IS WORSHIPED; SO THAT HE AS GOD SITTETH IN THE TEMPLE OF GOD SHOWING HIMSELF THAT HE IS GOD."

Sect. 2.—Temporal Power added to Spiritual Rule.

"These kings shall give their power unto the beast."

During all his exaltation in the church the pope had also been growing strong in the state.

In striving to follow him in his progress toward the sovereignty which he finally attained, we shall find Paul's prediction our best guide: "He who now hindreth will hinder until he be taken out of the way." The civil power of Rome, represented in the person of the emperor, was the great hindrance to the pope's advancement. His power increased just in proportion as that of the emperor "was taken out of the way."

1. By the conversion of Constantine this was done in one very important sense: the power of an enemy became that of a friend. By this change

much worldly dignity was added to the bishop of Rome.

2. By the transfer of the seat of government to Constantinople in the East, and to different cities in the West, the imperial power was also in a great measure literally "taken out of the way" in the city of Rome.

The first effect of the removal was, as we have seen, unfavorable to the pope's dignity, but in its ultimate result it promoted his attainment of temporal power.

The withdrawal of the imperial splendor and patronage diminished the reflected light which they had given him, but it also enabled him to shine in his own. It threw him into the second place with respect to his rival in the East, but it greatly increased his strength at home in the West. The supreme authority which had been exercised at Rome for a thousand years could not all be carried away by the departing emperor to the new city. That which remained must find a channel in which to flow; and although some of it was secured by the vicar of the city in the emperor's name, another portion readily coalesced with the spiritual dominion that had been rising there for three hundred years.

3. The authority of the emperor over Rome was diminished by distance and neglect. The pope was ever on the spot, ready to press his claims and to improve every opportunity for advancing his power.

4. The authority of the emperors was rendered precarious by the caprice that raised them to power, by their variable policy and the sudden, violent manner in which many of them were deposed or slain. The ecclesiastical government was steadfast; "the same character was assumed, the same policy was adopted by the Italian, the Greek, or the Syrian, who ascended the chair of St. Peter.[1] All were governed by one grand principle—the advancement of the see of Rome by all means and at all times. This gave to the administration of successive pontiffs the one kind of unity and consistency which the papal church has always possessed. It inspired confidence in the midst of confusion, and secured as permanent prerogatives all that carelessness or weakness yielded, all that superstition offered or that ignorance allowed.

5. The authority of the emperors declined with the strength of the empire. Their time was consumed in vain pursuits, and their resources, ex-

[1] Gibbon, III., p. 329.

torted by oppression, were lavished in luxury. The legions were enervated by inactivity, were invited to rebellion by relaxation of discipline, and fell in mutual slaughter on fields of civil strife. Much that the emperors thus lost the popes gained. They were freed from restraint; they became more conspicuous in proportion as greater lights were put out, and their dominion increased in vigor as knowledge sank into ignorance and religion degenerated into superstition.

6. When the Northern tribes descended on Rome they were in some degree restrained by reverence for its religion, to which many of them had professed a nominal conversion and yielded a partial obedience. Consequently, as their irruptions increased to a stream, a torrent, a flood, the authority of the pope was the only thing which they did not overwhelm. His intercession often averted danger; his protection shielded the oppressed; his wealth, sometimes left untouched amidst general pillage, ransomed the captive and relieved the distressed.

As the result of these causes, combined with his growing spiritual dominion, the Romans were gradually "accustomed to consider him as the first magistrate or prince of the city."[1] It would be impossible, we think, for any one to point out the moment, or the act, in which his *influence* over civil affairs passed into *authority and power.*

7. When, about the year 730, in the contest between the West and the East respecting the worship of images, the emperor forbade their worship, the pope aroused Rome and Italy to rebellion against him. Having triumphed in the struggle, "then at last (according to some writers) the Romans saluted the pope as their lord, and took an oath of allegiance to him." According to others, they at least acknowledged no other ruler, but yielded to him the sovereignty over them, in fact if not in form.

8. We have followed the bishop of Rome thus far in his progress toward the throne of temporal power. In his actual elevation on it we shall now see him sitting side by side with Charlemagne.

The royal authority in France had long been exercised by the mayor of the palace, nominally as the king's minister, but in fact as his master. Pepin, son of Charles Martel, dissatisfied with this precarious sovereignty, resolved to seize also the royal title. To render success certain, he sent

[1] Gibbon, III., p. 333.

to the pope, asking, "Who best deserved to be called king, he who held the power or he who had only the name?" Having obtained the answer that he desired, he assembled the estates of the realm and engaged his friends to propose that he should be declared king. They enforced their motion by announcing that it had the sanction of the pope. Then, without allowing time for deliberation, another party of his friends raised Pepin on a shield and proclaimed him king. The usurper, to give greater security to his dynasty, was anointed by the pope.

In return for these services he wrested from the Lombards the exarchate of Ravenna and the Pentapolis, and conferred them on the see of Rome. "The splendid donation was granted in supreme and absolute dominion, and the world beheld for the first time a Christian bishop invested with the prerogatives of a temporal prince."[1]

The grant was confirmed by Charlemagne, son of Pepin, who, having extended his conquests, was crowned by the pope EMPEROR OF THE WEST.

"The royal unction of the kings of Israel was dextrously applied; the pope assumed the cha-

[1] Gibbon, III., pp. 336–338.

racter of a divine ambassador; German chieftains were transformed into the Lord's anointed, and this Jewish title has been diffused and maintained by the superstition and vanity of modern Europe."

Thus, superadded to his spiritual authority and also upholding it, the temporal power of the pope was established simultaneously with the fiction of the divine right of kings.

9. And when both spiritual authority and temporal power—the slow growth of centuries and of manifold causes—had been fully grasped, a claim for them was set up by a daring stroke of falsehood and fraud, as if they had been original grants from Christ in heaven and Constantine on earth.

"Before the end of the eighth century some apostolic scribe, perhaps the notorious Isodore, composed THE DECRETALS and THE DONATION OF CONSTANTINE, the two magic pillars of the spiritual and temporal monarchy of the popes."[1]

By "the decretals," "that which had only lately been conceded or claimed, and with many conditions and protests, was announced under the sacred authority of Christian antiquity as an undoubted and divine right."[2]

[1] Gibbon.

[2] Hase's Ch. Hist., p. 185.

By "the donation" it was proclaimed that "Constantine withdrew from the see and patrimony of St. Peter, declared his resolution of founding a new capital in the East, and resigned to the popes the free and perpetual sovereignty of Rome, Italy and the provinces of the West.[1] "So deep were the ignorance and credulity of the times that this most absurd of fables was received with equal reverence in Greece and in France, and is still enrolled among the decrees of the canon law. In the revival of letters in the fifteenth century this fictitious deed was transpierced by the pen of Laurentius Valla. His contemporaries were astonished at his sacrilegious boldness; yet such is the progress of reason that before the next age the fable was rejected by the contempt of historians and poets, and the tacit or modest censure of the advocates of the Roman Church. The popes themselves have indulged in a smile at the credulity of the vulgar, but a false and obsolete title still sanctifies their reign; and by the same fortune which has attended the decretals and the Sybilline oracles, the edifice has subsisted after the foundations have been undermined."[2]

10. The way was now prepared for the assump-

[1] Gibbon, III., p. 339. [2] Ibid., pp. 339, 340.

tion of dominion over kings themselves. This soon became astounding, and reached its culmination in 1077, when Henry IV. of Germany, a successor of Charlemagne, in his contest with Hildebrand concerning the investiture of bishops, was excommunicated, deprived of the allegiance of his subjects, compelled to cross the Alps in the depth of winter, and, laying aside his diadem and robes, to stand barefoot three days at the barriers of a castle suing for admission, then to acknowledge the pope as his judge on whose decision hung his crown and kingdom; and finally, having fallen in the struggle, was pursued with maledictions after death and his body cast out of its grave.

Sect. 3.—Election to Office Wrested from the People by Kings and Popes.

"As being lords over God's heritage."

We have shown that in the republican churches established at the beginning of Christianity an apostle, the deacons, the bishops and other officers were elected by the people. During the transformation of the churches—as an essential part, indeed, of the transformation—restrictions were gradually laid on the privilege of election until it was, at last, taken utterly away. Some of the restrictions are clearly recorded in history, and traces are left of many more.

I. As bishops advanced in authority they began to control the election of those officers who were to be subordinate to them. "Already, from the third century, the deacons were no longer nominated by the members of the community, but by the bishops. Although it appears by the letters of Cyprian that, even in his time, no priest could be elected without the consent of the community, that election was far from being free. The bishop proposed to his parishioners the candidate whom he had chosen, and they were permitted to make such objections as might be suggested by his conduct and morals. They lost this last right toward the middle of the fourth century."[1]

II. As emperors and kings acquired influence in the churches, they too exercised it over the choice of officers.

When an election was contested their decision settled the dispute. When it was the scene of popular disturbance they interposed to quell the tumult and to control its cause. When they conferred dignity and wealth on an office they expected to nominate the candidate and to confirm

[1] Guizot, notes to Gibbon, vol. i., p. 525.

the election, if not to make the choice. "From the middle of the fourth century the bishops of some of the larger churches, particularly those of the imperial residence, were almost always chosen under the influence of the court, and were often and immediately nominated by the emperor."[1]

III. When ecclesiastical office became a centre of influence and power the sovereigns of the realm claimed jurisdiction over it. And in general, when it possessed any value, they seized it, as they did other things, either entirely for their own advantage or to strengthen the vassalage of their subjects, "as if these held everything from their sovereign lord and king."

The struggle between Henry IV. and Hildebrand for the right of investing bishops—involving as it did the independence of sovereigns in their own dominions or the supremacy of the pope over them as a king of kings—afforded also evidence that the free choice of the people in the election of the bishops had been taken away.

In view of these known facts and principles, we might venture to affirm that, by a process substantially similar, throughout the Roman empire and in the rising monarchies of Europe, elections grad-

[1] Planck, in notes to Gibbon, vol. i., p. 525.

ually passed from the people to the prelate, the emperor or the king.

But as the supremacy of the popes crowns the stupendous fabric of monarchical usurpation, like the dome of St. Peter's conspicuous from afar, it will be sufficient for us to mark the steps by which their election was wrested from the assembly of the church and placed actually in their own hands.

1. A decisive interference by the emperor occurred in the year 367, when a contested election of a pope had filled the city of Rome with confusion and arrayed the parties in bloody strife. Valentinian adjudged the office to one of the claimants and banished the other.[1]

2. A similar difficulty arose in 419, when Honorious not only decided between the rivals, but also commanded that whenever two persons were chosen a new election should be held.[2]

3. In 483, soon after the fall of the Western empire, Odoacer, the barbarian king of Italy, sent his lieutenant to the door of the church and arrested the voting which was in progress. He then commanded that in future no election should be held without the king or his deputy being

[1] Bower, I., p. 84. [2] Ibid., p. 162.

present to moderate the meeting and approve the choice.[1]

4. In 526, the city being divided into many parties, Theodoric, the Ostrogoth, appointed a person who had not been named among the candidates. This all resisted, but he prevailed on them to acknowledge his nominee, and ordained that henceforth no election should be valid unless it was confirmed by the king. This regulation extended to the election of all the bishops of Italy, and was continued in force by the other Gothic kings, and afterward by the Greek emperors when they again became masters of Italy.[2]

5. In 741, the Romans being in revolt and the emperor too weak to subdue them, Zachary was elected and consecrated without consulting him.[3]

Here let us take notice that, although it has not been possible to mark distinctly the pope's first act of internal temporal sovereignty over the people, this confirmation of his own election was a transition-point at which, with respect to the external power of the emperor, he ceased to be a subject and claimed to be a prince.

6. In 769 a council held at Rome decreed that henceforth no person should be eligible to the office

[1] Bower, I., p. 271 [2] Ibid., p. 327. [3] Ibid., II., p. 76.

of pope who had not previously passed through the inferior degrees to that of cardinal deacon or cardinal priest. This was the first actual restriction of the office to the cardinals.

7. When Charlemagne, in the year 800, confirmed the grant of temporal dominion to the popes he reassumed the right of approving their election.[1] Thus, in becoming princes, they seemed to subject themselves again to the emperor. But this was only apparent and transient—a winding of the stream around an obstacle, not a turning back of its onward flow. The right continued to be exercised by succeeding emperors, yet not without interruption and resistance, until the accession of Hildebrand in 1073.

He was the last pope whose election was submitted to the emperor for approval.

8. But before that time—in 1059—a more important restriction on the rights of the people was commenced by a decree that the election should be made by the college of cardinals alone, while the rest of the clergy, the people and the emperor should be allowed only to confirm the choice. This great stride encountered violent opposition, but was nevertheless successfully made.[2]

[1] Gibbon, III., p. 351. [2] Bower, II., p. 368.

9. In the following century—1179—the last daring step was taken. The election was vested absolutely in the cardinals, and all others were excluded from any concern in it whatever.[1]

While the darkness of the Middle Ages was yet unbroken, and when the double supremacy of Rome over church and state was at its height, the finishing hand was put to the domination by the decree that it should perpetuate itself. The pope creates the cardinals, and the cardinals elect one of themselves to be the pope.

[1] Mosheim Ch. Hist. Twelfth Century.

PART III.

The Republics of Modern Times.

"He hath made of one blood all nations of men to dwell on all the face of the earth."

CHAPTER I.

THE REAWAKENING OF THE NATIONS.

"He had in his hand a little book opened, and cried with a loud voice, as when a lion roareth."

IN order to understand the subject before us we must remember that, together with the rise of ecclesiastical power, there was a growing corruption of the Christian faith and life. The mystery at work from the beginning was a "mystery of iniquity" as well as of power. According to the inspired delineation of it, it was marked by want of love for the truth, by lying wonders and all deceivableness of unrighteousness.

Christianity indeed never changes. It is now just that which Christ and his apostles taught, and which the Scriptures record. But, under the name of corrupted Christianity, we have to do with the faith and practice of men in perversion of the Scriptures or in ignorance of them. As thus professed, the doctrines of Christianity were soon mingled with prevalent theories of philosophy, and with pagan, druidical and Saxon superstitions. Its code of morals, sound in principle, of universal application and requiring purity of life, was contaminated by deeply-rooted corruption and lawless violence. Its active agency for promoting the instruction of mankind, having thrown aside the panoply of truth, was overpowered by the ignorance of the nations it was sent to save.

Amidst the vast and intricate agencies which were combined in producing these results one fact sufficient for our purpose stands out to view: THE WORD OF GOD WAS WITHHELD AND WITHDRAWN FROM THE KNOWLEDGE OF MEN. This was at first the effect, and then in its turn the cause, of ignorance, error and evil. But whether cause or effect, it is the key to the mystery. In proportion as we follow the Scriptures going forth completed at the close of the first century, and mark the influences which limited and arrested their progress, we master the terrible problem involved in the corruption of Christianity.

Along the whole path the absence and banishment of the Scriptures appear in close conjunction with the rise of despotic power and the increase of dissolute living. And when, at length, a new zeal in the study and diffusion of the Scriptures is awakened, a struggle for liberty again accompanies the reaching after holiness and the search for truth.

During the eleventh, twelfth and thirteenth centuries, of which Hildebrand, Innocent and Boniface may serve as representatives, papal power ran to every excess of riot. But, like other rioters, it spent its substance and began to be in want.

Its usurpations goaded kings to madness, and they turned on their assailant. Its tyrannies drove the clergy to despair, and they rallied around their king. Its rival seats at Rome and Avignon divided its counsels, exposed its vices and poured contempt on its arrogant claims. By preaching the Crusades, it sent forth the nations in fanatical hordes or glittering hosts to rescue the manger and the tomb of Jesus. But the gigantic efforts were as waves against a rock. When, at length, Europe came to herself again, the enchanter's spell was broken, and the feudal institutions, the strongest bulwarks of despotism—like their own impregnable castles giving security to violence—were undermined and ready to fall.

These and other influences which contributed to disenthrall the nations have received patient investigation from many gifted minds. To comprehend them all would be the statesman's grandest work. It is our easier part to trace the popular energy aroused by the Scriptures; to mark its struggles with despotic power; its fall, deliverance, and, as we may hope, its approaching triumph.

Sect. 1.—The Huguenots in France.

"They said in their hearts, 'Let us destroy them together.'"

A heathen historian of the fourth century contrasts "the worldly pomp of the bishops of Rome, who alleged the grandeur of the city as their excuse, with the example of some bishops of provinces, who by their frugal diet, plain dress, modest look and pure lives approved themselves to the eternal God and all his true worshipers."

Such genuine Christians were to be found in many places of the provinces in every century following the apostolic age. Among them the Waldenses and Albigenses began, about the thirteenth century, to attract notice by their numbers, their adherence to the Scriptures and resistance to the doctrines and tyranny of Rome. The pope, having attempted in vain to suppress the heresy, stirred up the kings of France against them, who, at the head of crusading armies, put two hundred thousand to death. Their opinions, however, were not rooted out, but were driven to the mountains or spread abroad into many parts of Europe.

This persecution was the first of a series by which the French kings cut off out of their land those who feared God and took his word as their guide.

Again, at the beginning of the sixteenth century, Lefevre, Farel and Calvin, at the University of Paris, began to study and translate the Bible and spread abroad its truths. The nation was moved. Minds which the stirring events of the age had aroused, and which the revival of learning had trained to reflection, seized with avidity the reasserted doctrines. Many whom other influences had not reached were awakened by the preaching and writings of the Reformers. The Scriptures were eagerly sought after and read with delight. The supremacy of the pope was denied and the independence of the civil power affirmed. Republican churches were formed, and by their chosen representatives were united into a synod.

At first, Francis gave protection to the learned and eloquent men who were engaged in the work. Having a quarrel with the pope, he even thought of professing himself a Protestant. But it was whispered to him, "In that case you would be yourself the greatest sufferer: *a new religion requires a new prince.*" This hint appears to have decided him, and after his defeat and capture by Charles V. at the battle of Pavia he became a bitter persecutor. At the head of his court he went bareheaded to church, and while Protestants were being burned to death along the streets he knelt down to pray for himself and his kingdom. By his permission the retreats of the Albigenses were invaded, their towns burned, their fields ravaged and thousands of persons slain.

Henry II. followed in the steps of his father. As part of the festivities at his coronation he had many Protestants burned, the earnest of what he designed to do. Political affairs for a while engrossed his attention, and procured for the Reformation a brief respite. Soon, however, the storm raged more terribly than before. The Inquisition was established, the prisons were filled, and the king seemed to be planning the destruction of all his heretical subjects, when death cut him down.

His conduct must not be attributed to bigotry alone. The rise of the reformed religion necessarily became in its political aspect a struggle for liberty against absolute power. The reply made to

Henry by a distinguished military officer explains much of the opposition of kings to the religion of the Bible: "Sire, you can dispose of the offices I hold, my property and my life, but my soul is subject only to the Creator from whom I received it, *and whom, in this respect, it is my only duty to obey.*" To assert this principle is to spring a mine beneath every despotic throne.

The following reigns were under the control of the queen-mother and the Duke of Guise, whose mutual struggles and intrigues for the possession of absolute power gave additional rigor to despotism and aroused the utmost fury of persecution.

The Huguenot party, advancing in numbers and influence, became deeply involved in the contest for liberty. They were favored or denounced by the royal rivals, as the balance of power or the hope of supremacy required.

At length civil war arrayed the strength of the kingdom in hostile ranks, and many of those most distinguished by station, ability and character were slain. The Huguenots were defeated, and, after a short period of treacherous favor, their leaders were allured to Paris to celebrate the marriage of Margaret, the sister of the king, with Prince Henry of Navarre.

Then, on the 24th of August, 1572, ensued the massacre of St. Bartholomew, the result of counsels entered into by the pope, Catharine de Medici and her son, Charles IX.

The tolling of a bell at midnight was the signal. The Duke of Guise, leading on the troops and calling out that it was by the king's command, exhorted them to let none escape. Within the very walls of the palace nearly all were slain, and

> "copious as a thunder-shower,
> The blood of Huguenots through Paris streamed."

The dead were thrown from windows and tops of houses, were dragged along the streets and cast into the river. For three days the slaughter raged without abatement, and was prolonged in a less degree a whole week. It went farther than the plotters anticipated, cutting down not only the leaders of the Huguenots, but all ranks. It extended also by the king's command beyond the city into every part of France. In all, seventy thousand persons were slain. "When the pope heard the tidings he went in grand procession to his cathedral and ordered a Te Deum to be sung."

This atrocious deed was the climax of the second wholesale extermination of a class who, in a greater degree than any others in the land, combined the love of liberty with morality and religion.

At the close of the next century—1685—the edict of Nantes, by which Henry IV. granted religious liberty to his subjects, was revoked. *This led to a third general persecution, in which France lost half a milliom more of her best citizens, who were either slain or driven away to other lands.*

And so it came to pass that when, at the close of another century—1789—the horrors of the Revolution fell on her, when anarchy prevailed, terror reigned and despotism triumphed, these were simply the fruits of the previous slaughter and exile by which truth and righteousness had been cut off out of the land.

Sect. 2.—The Protestants in Germany.

"Out of weakness were made strong."

At the commencement of the fifteenth century, John Huss, a professor in the University of Prague, began to preach against the doctrines of the Roman church, the corruptions of the clergy and the supremacy of the pope. His learning, eloquence and purity of life, acting on the convictions of the people and on their longing for a better religion, produced a great commotion not only in the city, but throughout Bohemia. The clergy of all ranks were rendered odious. Their honors and advantages, their credit and authority, were in danger. They therefore rose against him and procured his martyrdom at the stake. But his opinions were lodged in the minds and hearts of multitudes, and his death inflamed their zeal and goaded them to madness. Persecuted and oppressed, they retired to a mountain and raised the standard of war in order to obtain liberty to worship God. The emperor put many of them to death in a barbarous manner, and on their part, also, great outrages were committed. They were ignorant of the gospel, their struggles to obtain a knowledge of it were opposed and their teachers put to death.

Yet they made progress. They studied the word of God more thoroughly, renounced their errors, sheathed the sword and expelled the disorderly from among them. Thus improved, they maintained their faith, and were ready for the coming of a brighter day.

A century after Huss, Martin Luther, at the University of Wittenberg, feeling after truth with a sincere and noble mind, found the Bible and learned from it that, being justified by faith, men have peace with God. He nailed his theses to the cathedral door, taught the truth in the university, preached it, wrote it and sent it, as on the wings of the wind, through Germany to every man's door. Caught up with friendly violence by the concealed hand of the elector of Saxony and placed in the castle of the Wartburg, he there translated the Scriptures, which soon were diffused as a flood of light through the land.

With many of the results which followed, though they be the noblest and most important, we are not now directly concerned. We have only to mark the movement produced among the people, the stimulating of their consciences and the strengthening of their determination to study the Bible for themselves, and to worship God according to its commands.

This brought them into collision with prelates and princes, with the emperor and the pope. Arbitrary power asserted dominion over the conscience; therefore, now, as in the first days of Christianity, obedience to the word of God was treason against the throne. The pope wrote thus to the emperor: "If I am called to be foremost in making head against the storm, it is not because I am the only one threatened, but because I am at the helm. The imperial authority is more invaded than even the dignity of Rome." "What!" exclaimed his legates to different kings, "will these presumptuous Germans pretend to decide points of faith in a national assembly? They seem to expect that kings, the imperial authority, all Christendom, the whole world, should bend to their decision."

The measures of the emperor for suppressing the Protestant cause soon became vigorous and decided. He hurried to a conclusion the war with France, made a truce with the Turks and an alliance with the pope.

He affirmed that he took up arms, not in a religious, but a civil quarrel, not to oppress any who continued quiet and dutiful, but to humble the arrogance of those who had thrown off subordination to him. The pope, on the other hand, declared that the real object of their confederacy was the maintenance of religious faith. This double assertion of the motives which influenced them shows that, in the impending contest, both civil and religious liberty were at stake.

Having assembled their troops, the Protestant princes published their manifesto, in which "they represented their conduct with regard to civil affairs as dutiful and submissive; they asserted religion to be the sole cause of the violence which the emperor meditated against them, declared their resolution to risk everything in the maintenance of their religious rights, and foretold the dissolution of the German constitution if the emperor should finally prevail against them."[1]

In reply, Charles published against them, without the consent of the diet, the ban of the empire, "the ultimate and most rigorous sentence which the German jurisprudence has provided for the punishment of traitors. By it they were declared rebels and outlaws, their goods were confiscated, their subjects absolved from allegiance, and it became not only lawful but meritorious to invade their territories."

They had, therefore, now only to choose between open hostilities and unreserved submission to the emperor's will. Accepting the former, they sent a herald to his camp with a declaration of war, renouncing all allegiance, homage or duty which he might claim or they had yielded hitherto.

Such was the origin of the conflict in which the triumphs of the emperor tended to increase despotic power, while the advantages gained by the Prot-

[1] Robertson's Charles V., Book VIII.

estants promoted liberty of conscience and the general rights of mankind.

"The treaty of Passau, in 1552, overturned the vast fabric in erecting which Charles had employed so many years, and had exerted the utmost effort of his power and policy. It annulled his regulations with regard to religion, defeated his hopes of rendering the imperial authority absolute and hereditary in his family, and established the Protestant church in Germany upon a firm and secure basis."[1]

Charles having resigned his dominions, Philip II. attempted to impose the inquisition on the Netherlands. This excited an insurrection the first fury of which raged against the images and decorations of the churches. In these outrages only the lowest classes of the people were engaged. They were impelled not by a passion for plunder, but by zeal to destroy what they considered objects of idolatrous regard. Motley says there is abundant evidence that they abstained entirely from robbery and left heaps of jewelry and plate lying unheeded on the ground. We lament and condemn their destructive course. It was, indeed, condemned at the time by the more enlightened, who exerted all

[1] Charles V., Book X.

their influence against it, and arrested it in two weeks. Yet we must remember that their religious leaders and guides, while they had trained them to offer idolatrous worship to many of these splendid works of art, had also kept all better instruction from them. Consequently, when they were awakened to perceive the guilt and folly of the idolatry, was it strange that their first blind impulse was to despise, to hate and to destroy?

Philip, maddened by these excesses, entered on the severest measures to destroy the Protestants. The Duke of Alva was sent against them with a powerful Spanish army, and for six years the country suffered all that a ferocious tyranny could inflict.

The Protestant cause found a wise and zealous defender in the Prince of Orange, who, assisted by the German princes and the English queen, rallied nearly all the provinces under his standard. The Duke of Alva, foiled in his efforts to subdue the country, was recalled.

When the Prince of Orange was assassinated, his son—only seventeen years old—was chosen in his stead. He became one of the greatest generals of the age, and during a career of forty years was illustrious for his military genius and success.

After the most heroic valor and endurance on the part of the people, continuing, with several intervals of truce, for seventy years, the independence of the country was secured.

In Bohemia also the persecution of the Protestants provoked a revolt. This was the beginning of a civil war throughout the empire that continued thirty years and drew into it the principal powers of Europe.

During a large part of this time the emperor's forces were commanded by the able and mysterious Wallenstein, and to him was opposed the illustrious Gustavus Adolphus, who about the middle of the war espoused the Protestant cause.

Both these generals perished in the contest, Gustavus in battle at the moment of victory, and Wallenstein by an assassin's hand. At length, in 1648, "after all parties had exhausted their resources and Germany was deluged with the blood of Spaniards, Hollanders, Frenchmen, Swedes, besides that of her own sons, the peace of Westphalia was concluded." By it freedom of worship was established, the smaller states were emancipated from the authority of the emperor, and his supremacy over the Germans was reduced to a shadow and a name.

Sect. 3.—The Reformers in Switzerland.

"*Rise and measure the temple of God, the altar and them that worship therein.*"

The independence of Switzerland, never completely lost, had been established by William Tell.

There was still aristocracy in its government; there was the exercise of arbitrary power, for power had not yet been taught to be of gentler mood; there was also the influence of surrounding kings, which their gold rendered doubly effective by drawing the Swiss into their armies, rending the land with factions and arraying brothers against each other in deadly strife.

Yet, with all these drawbacks, popular liberty had its home among the Alps, and when the Reformation began its course it found there facilities that nowhere else existed, and achieved results nowhere else in that day attained.

There a great part of Calvin's amazing life-work was performed. He instructed students, among whom were many celebrated men from various countries of Europe. He preached very constantly as one of the pastors of Geneva; wrote commentaries on nearly all the books of the Bible; was prominent in all the earnest disputations of his times; participated largely in the government of the church, and also of the city, for which his study of the civil law had abundantly qualified him; and corresponded incessantly with the Reformers and other distinguished men throughout Europe, directing thus the Reformation in Scotland and France, and exerting an important influence over it in England and other countries. "There was not a single day of his life in which he was faithless to his trust. Many a day he had no time to look up to the light of the sun, and many a night no time to sleep."[1]

The Reformation in Switzerland was indeed very far from being perfect. It was stern in its tone. It was not free from tyranny. Servetus was even burned for heresy at Geneva. This act "was cruel, it is indefensible, it was at the time impolitic. Yet it was the act of the council after long deliberation; it was in accordance with the laws of all the states of Europe" and with the spirit of the age. Both civil and religious liberty had been crushed under one despotism, against which men were now struggling. But they had not yet obtained liberty, much less had they rediscovered the Saviour's distinction between the things of Cæsar and those of God. That discovery would in time again be

[1] Prof. Henry B. Smith.

made, and through the influence of Calvin's teaching. But it was not made by Calvin himself. And, notwithstanding the one great crime, and many kindred imperfections with which the Reformers in Switzerland are to be charged, by them the germs were planted of "churches without a prelate and states without a king."

Sect. 4.—The Covenanters in Scotland.

"They wandered in mountains and dens and caves of the earth."

Christianity, perhaps, entered Scotland in the first century, but was certainly established there about the close of the third.

During the persecution which then raged throughout the Roman empire many Christians were driven from England into Scotland. They were kindly received, and were assigned a dwelling-place on the Isle of Man.

About the same time the Culdees—"Cultores Dei," worshipers of God—began to flourish. They steadfastly opposed the supremacy of the Romish church and adhered to the word of God.

In 565, Columba came from Ireland and established his missionary college on the island of Iona amidst the storms of the western coast,

"Where Christian piety's soul-cheering spark
(Kindled from heaven between the light and dark
Of time) shone like the morning star."

Rome began to seek control over Scotland in the fifth century, yet up to the close of the tenth the bishops who were introduced had no divided diocese or superiority over others, but governed the church in common with presbyters.

After the middle of the sixth century Romish usurpation greatly increased and the supremacy of the pope was acknowledged, yet there were frequent witnesses for the truth and against the corruptions of the Church of Rome.

At the opening of the fifteenth century the Reformation began to dawn. John Resby, an Englishman and scholar of Wycliffe, about 1407 was arrested and burned at the stake for denying the pope's supremacy. Ten years after, a Bohemian missionary suffered death at St. Andrews. Still later a new impulse was given to the work by the writings of the Reformers and by copies of Tyndale's New Testament, which found their way into the country. Hamilton and Wishart also, both of whom had studied on the Continent, preached boldly until they were arrested and burned.

These martyrdoms increased the determination

of the people and prepared the way for Knox, who, on his return from Geneva, prosecuted the Reformation with great vehemence and zeal.

In 1560 the Parliament established the Protestant faith on the model of Calvin and Geneva. The next year Mary "Queen of Scots" ascended the throne and attempted to restore Romanism. She was, however, resisted by Knox, the Parliament and the people, and soon fled into England. Protestantism was then again declared to be the only religion of Scotland.

James V. assumed power in his eleventh year. His policy was a mixture of tyrannical self-will and boyish submission to artful favorites. He both irritated and mortified his subjects, and was soon involved in disputes with the nobles, the clergy and the people. Becoming king of England on the death of Elizabeth, he arrayed himself against the struggle for liberty in two countries instead of one.

Sect. 5.—The Puritans in England.

"Thou must prophesy again before many peoples and nations and kings."

During the last half of the fourteenth century John Wycliffe, a professor of divinity in the University of Oxford, asserted the doctrine that the knowledge of God's revealed will is to be found in the Scriptures only, and by every man who earnestly and humbly seeks it.

He denied both the secular and spiritual jurisdiction of the papal court, and was opposed to the whole framework of the hierarchy as a device of clerical ambition. His industry was wonderful. He preached constantly, both at the university to the learned, and in his parish church to the common people. The number of brief tracts that he wrote baffles calculation. Two hundred are said to have been burned in Bohemia. His disciples, under the name of "poor priests," itinerated over the country, preaching in church-yards, markets and fairs.

In his writings and preaching the supreme authority of the Scriptures was explicitly maintained. Whatever he advanced he rested on their testimony. He made them familiar to the people by his abundant quotations, and at length translated them all into English, multiplying copies by the aid of transcribers, and by his poor priests diffusing them abroad.

The new doctrines insensibly acquired advocates and defenders among the higher classes. A spirit of inquiry was awakened, and the seed was sown of that religious revolution which in little more than a century astonished and convulsed the nations of Europe.

He died peacefully at his work. Stricken down by disease while officiating in his church, he never spoke again. But the council of Constance, pursuing him after death, condemned his writings, and decreed that his bones should be taken out of the ground and thrown far off from Christian burial.

"To Lutterworth they come," says Fuller, in his famous words, which have themselves been diffused abroad by historians, orators and poets, "take what was left out of the grave, burn them to ashes, and cast them into Swift—a neighboring brook, running hard by. *Thus this brook has conveyed his ashes into Avon, Avon into Severn, Severn into the narrow seas, they into the main ocean; and thus the ashes of Wycliffe are the emblem of his doctrine, which now is dispersed all the world over.*"

The fruits of Wycliffe's teaching appeared at the beginning of the following century, when the inheritors of his opinions, under the new name of Lollards, again awoke the cry of reformation.

A statute was passed against them, denouncing them for holding unlawful conventicles and schools, writing books, wickedly instructing the people and stirring them to sedition. The prisons were filled, various punishments were inflicted, and for the first time the fires of Smithfield were lighted. This persecution continued until the Wars of the Roses, in the latter half of the century, when "the storm was their shelter."

During the earlier part of Henry VIII.'s reign the papal religion was maintained with all the strength of royal authority. His majesty even wrote against Luther, and thus gained from Leo X., in 1521, the title of "Defender of the Faith." But when the pope refused to divorce him from Catharine of Arragon he renounced his jurisdiction and transferred the supremacy over the church to himself. Henry consented to a partial reformation of religion, and gave the word of God to the people, that he might thus prevent their return to Rome. He broke up the monasteries, not because of their corruptions, but that he might seize on their revenues. "Although he had thrown off the authority of the Roman pontiff, he had no notion that the English church should be left without a pope. His objection was not to the thing but to the person, and his main object evidently was that, in so far at least as the religion of his own subjects was concerned, he might mount the same seat of absolute authority himself. The ancient head of the Roman church never put forward greater pretensions to infallibility than were, if not distinctly advanced in words, yet constantly acted on by the new head of the English church, in his narrower empire of spiritual despotism."[1] He "seemed to think that his subjects owed an entire resignation of their reasons and consciences to him; and as he was highly offended with those who still adhered to papal authority, so he could not bear the haste that some were making to a further reformation before or beyond his allowance."[2]

During the brief reign of Edward VI., when the English Reformers, because of the king's minority and piety, were at liberty to follow their own judgment, the most important progress was made. Then it was that the "Calvinistic" articles of religion were prepared and published.

The character of the next reign, of its persecutions and results, is represented by the familiar phrase, "Bloody Mary." The epithet has been branded indelibly on the memory of the queen, yet it belongs also to her husband—the cruel persecu-

[1] Pictorial History of England, vol. ii., p. 697.

[2] Bishop Burnett.

tor of many lands—to her ministers and to the spirit of the age.

But, with regard to this persecution, it has been well said that "Providence ordered that it should prepare the way for a popular and spiritual movement in the subsequent reign. It was not until the fires of Smithfield were lighted that great spiritual ideas took hold of the popular mind and the intense religious earnestness appeared which has so often characterized the English nation."[1]

At the accession of Elizabeth, Protestantism was re-established. "She had been bred up with a hatred of the papacy and a love for the Reformation; but as her first impressions in her father's reign were in favor of such old rites as he had retained, so in her own nature she loved state and some magnificence in religion as well as in everything else. She thought that in her brother's reign they had stripped it too much of external ornaments and had made their doctrine too narrow in some points."[2]

Entertaining these views, she interposed her authority to arrest the Reformation at such a point between popery and Protestantism as in her

[1] Lord's Mod. Hist., chap. v. [2] Burnett.

opinion was the proper "via media," and to establish it there for ever. "There were men among the clergy who were opposed, among other things, to the claims of the bishops to be considered a superior order to presbyters, and to have the sole right of ordination and exercise of ecclesiastical discipline; to the temporal dignities annexed to the episcopal office; to the prohibition in the public service of prayers composed by the clergyman himself; to the appointment of ministers by presentations from the crown, the bishops and lay patrons, instead of by the election by the people."[1] "The greater part of the clergy positively objected to the use of the surplice, including all the leading men, who were for simplifying the church ceremonial, in that and other respects, according to the Genevan model. Archbishop Parker stood almost alone with the queen in her determination to uphold it unaltered."[2]

This prelate and others, having been appointed commissioners by the queen, summoned the clergy of the several dioceses before them, and suspended all who refused to subscribe an agreement to submit to the queen's injunctions in regard to habits, rites and ceremonies. Great numbers of ministers,

[1] Pict. Hist. of Eng. [2] British Critic.

including many of those most eminent for their zeal, piety and popularity as preachers, were thus ejected from the service of their cures and sent forth into the world destitute of support. When they published a vindication of their opinions, an order was issued that no person should print or publish, bind or sell, any book against the queen's injunction.

Thus cast out of the church, the nonconformists assembled in private houses or elsewhere to worship God according to their own consciences. This practice gave the queen and her commissioners abundant employment in putting down conventicles. Offenders were arrested and punished in great numbers. When Archbishop Grindall recommended mild measures, the queen suspended him from his see and shut him up in his own house. The House of Commons having taken into consideration several measures for restraining the power of the church, she sent to tell them how highly she was offended by their daring to encroach on her supremacy and attempting what she had already forbidden. She also commanded the speaker to see that no bills touching reformation in matters ecclesiastical should be exhibited. These facts are specimens of that "strong Tudor arm by which she kept in decent bounds" both the clergy and the representatives of the people.

When James I. ascended the English throne he declared that he would allow no toleration, but would have one doctrine, one discipline, one religion in substance and in ceremonies. He curtly expressed his views in the maxim, "No bishop, no king;" and afterward said, with still more point, "If you aim at a Scottish presbytery, it agreeth with monarchy as God with the devil."

Such an opening indicated the character of his reign and foreshadowed the struggle between liberty and despotism, "between royal prerogatives and popular freedom," which was prolonged with increasing intensity throughout the seventeenth century, and resulted in the execution of Charles I., the temporary establishment of the commonwealth and the permanent weakening of the throne.

Sect. 6.—The Martyrs in Spain.

"That were slain for the word of God and for the testimony which they held."

Christianity was introduced into Spain at least as early as the second century, and at the beginning of the fourth it had filled the land.

At the fall of the Western empire the Goths conquered Spain, but as they were Christians they did not disturb its religion.

In the eighth century the finest parts of the kingdom were conquered by the Saracens, and the Crescent expelled the Cross. But the Christians obtained toleration as a sect, and from the mountains of the North maintained during seven hundred years a struggle for Christianity, their national independence and representative government.

With the success of the native princes in gradually reconquering the country their prerogative and the claims of the hierarchy also advanced.

In 1492 the crowns of Arragon and Castile were united by the marriage of Ferdinand and Isabella. The Moors were driven from Spain, the monarchy became strong, and papal supremacy, often protested against, was made sure.

The Inquisition was established by Ferdinand at the instigation of the priesthood and with the reluctant consent of Isabella. Designed at first chiefly to suppress heresy among the Jewish and Moorish converts, it became a government of terror that dictated terms to the king himself, trampled on imperial authority and crushed all freedom of thought in church and state.

The Reformation was introduced into Spain chiefly among the followers of Charles V. in his migrations from Germany. It was enthusiastically embraced by many, and, if it had been left unrestricted by royal authority, would have prevailed everywhere.

But Charles, and afterward Philip, through the Inquisition, silenced the arguments of the Protestants by throwing into prison those suspected of heresy and by burning them alive. The auto-da-fe was made a magnificent spectacle, grander than a bull-fight, at which the king and his court were seated in state.

According to Llorente, thirteen thousand perished thus up to the era of the Reformation, and a larger number in subsequent years, while hundreds of thousands pined in dungeons, had their property confiscated and suffered various tortures—tortures of soul as well as of body—and often worse than death at the stake.

By this process Protestantism was at length suppressed and the country reduced to abject submission to both royal and papal power. Yet in all parts of the peninsula germs of hostility to both remained. These were to bear fruit in subsequent times.

Sect. 7.—The Unawakened in Italy.

"She has glorified herself and lived deliciously."

In Italy, the assumed centre of Christianity, the Reformation made little progress. The power of the movement in France, Switzerland and Germany could not indeed be without influence even in Rome. But its effects there were superficial and easily suppressed, because the very elements of virtue had been corrupted and the foundations of faith dissolved. The common people were sunk into the lowest ignorance and superstition; the higher classes were scoffing infidels.

It was a characteristic of good society to dispute the fundamental principles of Christianity. No one was esteemed an accomplished man unless he entertained some heterodox opinions concerning religion. At court they spoke of the institutions of the church, of passages of Scripture and mysteries of religion in tones of derision. At the very moment when the priests were offering the sacrifice of the mass they blurted out blasphemies in denial of it.

In Italy the revival of learning, which was so striking a feature of the times, was a revival only of the ancient heathenism, philosophy and art.

There was no study of the Scriptures accompanying it, no inquiry after religious truth.

Rankè has pointed out this fact and placed it in strong contrast with the earnestness of the German scholars. "The development of the age led to an opposition against the church on both sides of the Alps. Beyond them it was connected with literature and science; on this side it arose out of spiritual studies and a profounder theology. There it was negative and incredulous; here it was positive and believing. There it abrogated the very basis of the church; here it re-established it. There it was mocking, satirical and pliantly submissive to power; here it was full of earnestness and deep indignation, and rose up against the Roman church, turning upon it the boldest attack it ever sustained."[1]

This state of things in Rome and Italy was the appropriate fruit of the papal system. On the other hand, because of this state of things around the popes, they could be notoriously wicked and worldly without exciting any outcry against the incongruity.

For these reasons we may regard the three popes at the threshold of the sixteenth century as repre-

[1] History of the Popes, Book I., chap. ii.

senting all ranks of society over which they were the head, and as furnishing an explanation of the fact that, with the Reformation all around them, Rome and Italy were not reformed.

Alexander VI., the first of the three, was a monster of wickedness. We cannot always distinguish between what he did personally and what he allowed Cæsar Borgia to do. "On all remarkable occasions of death men thought immediately of poisoning by the pope." And his own death was actually by poison, which he had ordered to be administered to one of the cardinals, but the cardinal contrived to have it set before the pope himself. Such was the manner in which he departed to his final account.

Julius II. waged bloody wars for the simple purpose of extending his worldly power. "He looked to the tumult of a general war with the highest hopes of gain, and desired to be lord and master of the game of the world. He led his troops in person, and in the hot war that ensued laid the foundation of a power such as no pope before him had possessed."[1]

Thus the way was prepared for the brilliant but transient day of Leo X., the child of fortune, as

[1] Ranke.

he has been called, and the man of the world. He was crowned with a splendor rivaling that of the old emperors. Squandering with lavish hand the treasure amassed by his predecessor, he replenished it with Tetzel's gold and many similar devices. And when Luther's voice against indulgences resounded through Europe, Leo was as one clothed in purple and faring sumptuously every day. The magnificence of his table exceeded that of kings. "For him men of genius wrote their plays. For him Raphael filled galleries and chapels with ideals of human beauty. The palace rang with music—the voice of harpers and musicians, of pipers and trumpeters—and he hummed the airs that were played. He passed the autumn in rural recreations, hawking, hunting and fishing; and in these was accompanied by improvisatori and other men of quick, light talent, capable of enlivening every hour of the day. In winter he returned to the city that was made merry by busy tradesmen and splendid by proficients in every art. Never had the court been more animated, cheerful and intellectual. No cost was too great for spiritual or secular festivals, plays and theatrical entertainments, presents and favors. Nothing was spared."[1]

[1] Ranke.

One evening, at his villa, Leo received tidings that the city of Milan had been taken by his troops, combined with those of the emperor. Rejoicing and triumphant, he continued walking to and fro between the fire on the hearth and the open window, watching the bonfires of the people outside. He then returned to Rome, and before the celebration of the victory was ended, without time to receive "the last rites of the church," he passed away from earth, a victim either of malarious air or, as was suspected, of poisoned food. The populace followed him to the grave with jeers. "You sneaked in like a fox," they said, "ruled like a lion, and have gone off like a dog."

Is it strange that, although the Reformation was all around her, Italy was not reformed?

We have now traced the effect of the reasserted Scripture doctrine in arousing among the principal nations of Europe a determined pursuit of religious liberty. We have also seen that this was met with an equally determined resistance by arbitrary power. But although the various national elements that entered into the conflict may be separately considered, they were scarcely separate in action and influence. The same truth was employed everywhere in attacking one system of error, which was widely diffused among minds substantially alike. Hence there was a uniformity of result amidst variety, and a striving after essential agreement even when contradiction and strife appeared. Bonds of brotherhood were established among people of different countries. The strong sent assistance to the weak. Correspondence was instituted among minds of the highest order concerning the grandest themes. Strangers from distant regions were transformed to friends by common sufferings and joys. The exiles of France found refuge in Bohemia; those of the Netherlands in England; those of England and Scotland in Germany and Switzerland. Geneva became a centre of influence on all Europe, where the intellect of Calvin wrought out the principles of liberty for the state as well as of religion for the church.

There was unity also in the resistance made to the advancement of liberty. Charles V. and Francis I., covering their enmity under the semblance of friendship, joined in alliance against the heretics. Philip II., Catharine de Medici and the pope met in council to plan a general massacre throughout Christendom. Catholic Spain arrayed all her strength to overwhelm Protestant England.

Most marvelous of all the agencies for restoring the pope's supremacy and giving unity to them all, was the Order of the Jesuits. "One starlit night —August 15, 1534—on the summit of Montmartre, near Paris, seven young men, of whom Ignatius Loyola was the master-spirit, bound themselves together by the usual monastic vows, and added a special pledge of obedience to the pope." This association gradually assumed the form of the Society of Jesus. When the plan of it was presented to the pope, he exclaimed, "The finger of God is in it!"

To us, on the contrary, in view of all its results, it seems a striking instance of that "energy of Satan" which has given success to the papacy from the beginning.

"Before the death of Loyola his followers had secured the most important chairs in the universities of Europe, and had become confessors to the most powerful monarchs, teachers in the best schools and preachers in the principal pulpits. They had become an organization which could outwatch Argus with his hundred eyes and outwork Briareus with his hundred arms. It had forty thousand eyes open on every cabinet and private family in Europe, and forty thousand arms extended over the necks of both sovereigns and people. It had become a mighty power in the world, inseparably connected with the education and the religion of the age, the prime mover of all political affairs, the grand prop of absolute monarchies, the last hope of the papal throne."[1]

By these and other influences the people of Europe were drawn slowly, on the one hand, into unity of feeling and purpose, while on the other, storms of war, excited by royal and papal tyranny and strife, shrouded them in darkness and drenched them in blood.

In the mean time a new hemisphere had been discovered, and to it the working out of liberty for mankind was transferred.

[1] Lord's Mod. Hist., chap. ix.

CHAPTER II.

THE REPUBLICS OF THE NEW WORLD.

"To the woman were given two wings of a great eagle, that she might fly away into the wilderness."

THAT a new era in the development of divine Providence was at hand might have been inferred from the accumulation of events fitted to change the face of the world.

The fall of Constantinople, by which the Eastern empire was subjected to the despotism of the false prophet; the revival of Hebrew and Greek literature, by which the restoration of God's word to Europe, and eventually to all nations, was secured; the invention of printing, which would bring human and divine knowledge within the reach of all men; the birth of Tyndale, Luther, Zwingli, Farel, Calvin, Cranmer and Knox, who were to be among the principal agents in rediffusing Christianity; and THE DISCOVERY OF AMERICA, by which a broad land was opened for civil and religious liberty,—all were clustered together within the period of sixty years—between 1450 and 1510.

Sect. 1.—North America Reserved as the Domain of Liberty.

The providence of God was signally displayed in preserving North America comparatively free from inhabitants, while the principal regions of the other hemisphere were at a very early period filled with vast hordes of strong, barbarous, impetuous men.

From the valley of the Nile, the shores of the Mediterranean, Central Asia and Northern Europe have issued forth a succession of warriors, filling the Eastern world with devastation and death. But when America was peopled, as is supposed from Asia, the tide of emigration passed down the western coast, and accumulated chiefly in the southern portion of the continent.

The "sons of the forest" who came east of the Mississippi were comparatively few in number—in Virginia, for example, about one to the square mile—and although brave and addicted to war, they rushed not on in impetuous masses, marched not in the locked array of the phalanx or the legion, but threaded their way in "Indian file." Their mode of warfare consequently had perils and horrors peculiar to itself, yet it was the only mode which the colonists could hope to withstand. If they had been attacked by dense masses, they must have been overwhelmed.

When Columbus landed on the New World it was at the Bahamas, not at the Chesapeake or the Delaware. The cry of the Spaniards being for gold, the natives pointed them to the *south*, not to the *north*. This ensured the establishment of their empire—which was to be characterized by blood, popery and despotism—over Mexico and South America, rather than over the northern portions of the continent. Afterward their determined efforts to establish themselves from the Carolinas to the Mississippi were defeated, and St. Augustine remained their northern limit on the Atlantic coast.

Thus was North America reserved almost unbroken by European colonies until the beginning of the seventeenth century, the precise time at which it had become possible on the one hand, and necessary on the other, that a decisive movement in behalf of civil and religious liberty should be made.

The French colonies at the Gulf of St. Lawrence were not established until about 1661—more than half a century after the foundations of Jamestown had been laid.

Under skillful leaders, aided by able Jesuit missionaries, they extended their settlements over Canada, across the lakes and down the Mississippi to its mouth. Taking possession of the most important points, they established a chain of forts between themselves and the English along the whole frontier line. For a time it seemed inevitable that the conflicts between France and England and between Catholics and Protestants would be reproduced over a broader territory in America. But the danger, happily, was terminated within the first century of colonial history. Four French and Indian wars were waged, the first beginning in 1690, and the last ending in 1759 with the capture of Quebec and the subjection of the French.

"This victory," says Bancroft, "one of the most eventful in the annals of mankind, gave to the English tongue and the institutions of the Germanic race the unexplored and seemingly infinite west and north."

Sect. 2.—General Causes which Promoted Republican Institutions.

In the colonies where the English language and laws prevailed, republican institutions were the natural result of the circumstances in which the colonists were placed, combined with the principles which they professed.

The providence of God led them to this land in associations formed on substantially equal terms and pledging mutual advantages. Common dangers and sufferings, common wants and pursuits exerted a powerful influence in uniting them together, and ensured a strong infusion of republican feeling in whatever form of government they might adopt.

The broad ocean between them and their former homes greatly diminished the royal control over them, and enabled them to act in many important matters according to their own choice.

Some of the colonies had governors appointed by the king, but the majority were under charter or proprietary governments. As the crown did little to aid in their settlement, so it had little right of interference in their affairs. Many of the laws were oppressive, and arbitrary restrictions were imposed on manufactures and commerce. But some of these could be evaded and others could not be enforced.

As early as the middle of the seventeenth century the colonists began to insist that they should not be taxed without their own assent, and that

Parliament had no authority over their internal affairs.

In general, only those persons came to America who loved liberty well enough to brave the ocean and live in a wilderness in order to obtain it. They would therefore choose popular institutions. "If," said William Penn, "we could not assure people of an easy, free and safe government, both with respect to their spiritual and worldly prosperity—that is, an uninterrupted liberty of conscience, and an inviolable possession of their civil rights and freedoms by a just and wise government—a mere wilderness would be no encouragement." "The colonies," says Bancroft, "were established and strengthened mainly by a succession of persons who fled from the distractions, civil strifes and religious persecutions of the times. The spirit of political freedom was strongly developed among them, and republican ideas and feelings, transmitted from the period of the Commonwealth in England, were widely diffused."

Nor must we fail to take notice of the fact that land was freely and largely distributed among the original settlers, and afterward could be easily acquired. This furnished a broad and secure foundation for republican institutions on which all could build, the wisest according to their plans, and the most ignorant "better than they knew."

Sect. 3.—Influence of the Scriptures in Producing these Causes.

Such being the general causes which combined to establish republicanism in America, we have now to show the influence which the Scriptures exerted in producing the causes themselves.

(1.) The Love of Liberty.

The love and pursuit of liberty which prompted and sustained the colonies were in a great measure owing to the Scriptures. These, as we have seen, had been widely diffused and zealously taught through many countries of Europe, and had aroused, enlarged and enlightened the public mind. They even who, in coming to America, sought mainly an increase of worldly prosperity, were strongly imbued with the love of liberty, and had derived it, partly at least, from the Bible.

(2.) The Character and Emigration of the English Puritans.

The settlement of New England must be ascribed entirely to the influence of religion and of the Scriptures.

A determination to secure for themselves and their descendants a pure and free worship of God according to the directions of his revealed word was the motive which brought the Pilgrim Fathers to America. "Their enterprise began from God. A solemn fast was held. 'Let us seek from God,' they said, 'a right way for us, our little ones and our substance.' 'I charge you before God,' said their minister, 'that you follow me no farther than you have seen me follow the Lord Jesus Christ. The Lord has more truth yet to break forth out of his holy word.'"[1] With similar views other settlers followed, "in order to form, in the New World, Protestant institutions, to countervail the Jesuit establishments already existing there, and to embrace for themselves and their brethren the secure asylum which had been furnished by the hand of divine Providence itself."[2]

This motive continued to be the prevailing one in the settlement of the other New England colonies.

Hume ascribes to the Puritans three marked peculiarities: In politics, they maintained the highest principles of civil liberty; in discipline, they opposed the ceremonies of the established

[1] Bancroft. [2] Ibid.

church; in doctrine, they defended the system of the first Reformers.

Such were the men who formed the chief portion of the settlers in New England, and such the controlling impulses by which they were moved. "They were formal and precise in their manners, singular in their forms of legislation and rigid in the observance of their principles. Every topic of the day found a place in their extemporaneous prayers and in their long and frequent sermons. But if from these outside peculiarities, which so easily excite the sneer of the superficial observer, we look to the genius of the sect itself, Puritanism was religion struggling for the people."[1]

(3.) Of the French Huguenots.

The French Huguenots, like the Puritans, were brought to this country by their devotion to civil and religious liberty.

Their first attempt to settle in America was made under the auspices of Admiral Coligny in 1562, ten years before the massacre of St. Bartholomew. Having discovered one of the finest harbors on the Atlantic coast, they named it Port Royal, and the whole district, for which they held

[1] Bancroft.

a charter from Charles IX., they called Carolina. But their colony did not succeed.

Sixty years later a considerable number settled in and around the city of New York, and after the revocation of the edict of Nantes, in 1685, many more found refuge in America, settling in various parts of the country.

No class of emigrants, in proportion to their numbers, contributed more than the Huguenots to the prosperity, intellectual progress and refinement of the United States. They were, almost without exception, persons of superior social standing and good education, yet they had also become accustomed to labor during the reverses which persecution and exile brought on them. In Virginia their flourishing farms were the wonder of the country. In South Carolina they established magnificent plantations on the banks of the Cooper. Wherever they settled they introduced important improvements in agriculture and manufactures, and in commerce they were among the most active and successful.

They were noted also for severe morality, great charity and polished manners. Their relative superiority may in some degree be measured by the fact that of seven presidents of Congress during the Revolution three were of Huguenot descent—Henry Laurens of South Carolina, John Jay of New York and Elias Boudinot of New Jersey—all of whom were eminent for ability, culture, integrity and devotion to liberty.

(4.) Of the Friends.

The "Friends"—or "Quakers," as they are often called—constituted a third division of colonists who came to America, mainly in pursuit of religious liberty.

Originating as a sect during the stormy days of the Commonwealth, they suffered much vexatious and cruel persecution on account of their marked peculiarities and rigid adherence to their principles. Many of them fled to the colonies. In New Jersey and Rhode Island they became strong, and under William Penn founded also the great central commonwealth which perpetuates his name.

Sect. 4.—Continued Influence of the Scriptures in the Colonies.

All these, and others, of various religious opinions, who were impelled to America by the principles of the Bible, persevered after their arrival in adhering to it as their guide.

The authorized English version, made by an assemblage of eminent scholars under the auspices of James I., had been published in 1611, only a few years before the embarkation of the Puritan colony. This coincidence was one of the links in the chain of God's providence over America. By it a version eminently fitted to be national and permanent was provided, just at the time when a colony distinguished for attachment to the Scriptures was about to give character to the Western world.

This Bible was diffused more and more widely. It has filled the land, and is to this day adopted, with only slight modification on the part of some, by all Protestant denominations, as a standard version, subject always to appeal to the original Scriptures.

From the beginning it was read by the people free from restraint imposed by king or magistrate. It became the family Bible, was read, expounded and preached in the churches and taught in the schools. Thus it exerted incessantly a forming influence on the language, culture, character and opinions of the people.

It was also received by the Puritans as the guide for civil government as well as the rule for private life. This portion of their creed has often been derided and condemned, yet if it be restricted to the principles of government, as distinguished from particular details, time has proved it to be correct.

Sect. 5.—Development of Republican Principles.

While the germs of American institutions were planted at the beginning, the development of them must be sought for in all our history up to the present moment, and onward into distant times. Bearing this in mind, we may take notice of some marked resemblances between the principles embodied in them and those taught in the Scriptures.

I. The independence of religion.

The Scriptures, as we have shown in former chapters, maintain that religion is of right independent of the civil power.

This doctrine was not at first generally understood even by those who fled to America in order to escape persecution. In Virginia the Church of England was established by law, and the supremacy of the king over it maintained.

The Puritans came to New England to secure the undisturbed enjoyment of their own religious opinions, in which, at the time, they were unanimous, but they were unwilling to admit any of contrary views to live among them. Like Calvin at Geneva, they regarded the state as included in the church. This theory led to the banishment of many persons on account of their religious opinions, and even to the death of a few. The law, however, which ordained the last-mentioned punishment, must be regarded as the dying struggle of the persecuting doctrines which had drawn their life from the Old World, but were not destined to live in the New. It was carried by a majority of one vote, and after sentence under it had been pronounced the fourth time, public opinion rose against it, and it was enforced no more.

When Maryland was settled, Lord Baltimore, a Roman Catholic, who had, however, been brought up a Protestant, granted toleration to all Christians. We honor this as being in advance of the age and nobly opposed to the spirit which ecclesiastical despotism had diffused through Europe. Lord Baltimore is fairly entitled to the honor of having been among the first who approached the true scriptural doctrine concerning religious liberty. Yet *the right* of the civil magistrate to interfere in religious matters he still asserted and maintained. While he granted toleration to all Christians, blasphemy against the Christian religion he declared to be punishable with death, and minor degrees of disrespect with slighter penalties.

In 1631, three years before the Maryland colony was planted, Roger Williams, a minister thirty years of age, who afterward joined the Baptists, arrived at Boston and advanced the memorable proposition THAT THE CIVIL MAGISTRATE HAS NO RIGHT TO RESTRAIN OR DIRECT THE CONSCIENCES OF MEN, AND THAT ANYTHING SHORT OF UNLIMITED TOLERATION FOR ALL RELIGIOUS SYSTEMS IS CONTRARY TO THE TEACHING OF JESUS CHRIST.

This sentiment caused his banishment from Massachusetts, and drove him without shelter into the forest. Having obtained land from the Indians, he named his settlement PROVIDENCE.

Surely the period well deserves to be kept in remembrance as a remarkable one in the providence of God.

"At a time when Germany was the battle-field for all Europe in the implacable wars of religion; when Holland was bleeding with the anger of vengeful factions; when France was still to go through the fearful struggle with bigotry; when England was gasping under the despotism of intolerance; more than forty years before William

Penn became an American proprietary,—Roger Williams asserted the great doctrine of intellectual liberty. He was the first person in modern Christendom to advance in its plenitude the doctrine of the liberty of conscience, the equality of opinions before the law. He was willing to leave Truth alone in her own panoply of light, believing that if, in the ancient feud between her and Error, the employment of force could be entirely abrogated, she would have much the best of the bargain."[1]

From that time his doctrine—one of the first principles announced by Christ and one of the last understood by his disciples—took deep root in America. Afterward, at the settlement of Pennsylvania, William Penn also guaranteed the rights of conscience. And at length, by an amendment to the Federal Constitution, it was ordained "*that Congress should make no law respecting the establishment of religion or prohibiting the free exercise thereof.*"

By a process so gradual did the independence of religion become a fundamental principle in American institutions.

[1] Bancroft.

II. The right of the people to govern themselves.

According to the New Testament, believers have the right to associate themselves as a church, having officers elected by themselves and being independent of all other churches except as they see proper to enter into alliance with them.

In like manner, in America, citizens are associated into communities, having their own officers, and being independent of all others, except as they have voluntarily united with others, and have consequently taken on themselves obligations, express or implied.

The first American republic was formed on board the Mayflower after the colonists had discovered that they were out of the limits of their patent, and therefore had not even its imaginary authority for taking possession of the land. Not even the shadow of the feudal fiction was to touch them on Plymouth Rock, "*as if*" the right to it "had been conferred by their sovereign lord, the king."

They signed a written constitution of government, declared themselves a body politic, resolved to enact laws and elected a governor to serve for a year. "When they landed their institutions were already perfected. Democratic liberty and independent Christian worship at once existed in America."

The first representative assembly was convened in Virginia in 1619. In Massachusetts, at first, the legislature comprised the whole body of the people, but in 1634, as the population increased, the representative system was adopted. So early did that system become "epidemic in America."

After other colonies had been founded in New England, their common interests soon bound them together in a union which was the germ of American confederation.

When British oppression threatened all the colonies, Massachusetts proposed that a congress of deputies should meet. The proposition was favorably received, and deputies from nine colonies assembled at New York. When the ministers of the crown persisted in their measures, Massachusetts again called on the other colonies requesting their united aid. When the Port Bill was passed they rallied in her defence. Virginia appointed a day of fasting and prayer, and proposed that a general congress should again assemble. To this Massachusetts responded by appointing her delegates and naming the day. The other colonies also assented, and the Continental Congress met at Philadelphia, thereby constituting a union of the colonies.

In May, 1775, citizens of Mecklenburg County, North Carolina, a community of Scotch and Irish descent and of Presbyterian doctrine and government, passed resolutions "dissolving the political bands which had connected them with the mother-country, absolving themselves from all allegiance to the British crown, declaring themselves a free and independent people, and pledging to each other, in support of their declaration, their mutual co-operation, their lives, their fortunes and their most sacred honor."

These resolutions are fairly entitled to rank among the earliest public expressions in favor of independence, and evidently furnished some of the noblest clauses in the immortal Declaration written by Jefferson, adopted by Congress, and published on the Fourth of July, 1776.

While the public mind was excited by the discussions which resulted in the Declaration of Independence, Thomas Paine addressed a tract, entitled "Common Sense," to the American people, strongly urging them to the adoption of such a measure. One of his prominent arguments was drawn from the opposition of the Scriptures to monarchical government, as evinced in the Jewish commonwealth and in the protest which the Prophet Samuel entered by divine command against the popular determination to have a king. From this we learn that, while the public sentiment of the American people had been to a great extent formed under the influence of confidence in the Bible as the word of God, even the author of the "Age of Reason" obtained from the same source some of his best arguments in favor of liberty.

The union established by the appointment of the Congress was strengthened by the "Articles of Confederation," and, after the Revolution was perfected, by "the people of the United States, ordaining and establishing THE CONSTITUTION."

3. NATIONAL UNITY.

It has often been asked, In what mind did the glorious idea originate of ONE NATION, to be formed of the independent sovereignties which were scattered over the country?

There can no one answer be given to this question. As well might we ask, In what instant was the oak matured? The idea of American unity was coeval with the founding of the colonies. It grew with their growth and strengthened with their strength.

But the Scriptures contain as models both the Jewish state and the Christian church. In the state we see a people who were divided into tribes. The tribes consisted of families and the families of individuals; yet by the possession of a common country their unity as a nation was secured without the division into tribes being destroyed, or the union of families disturbed, or the rights of individuals forgotten.

In the church, as we have shown in a previous chapter,[1] a similar unity existed—"one formed of many." This had its centre and source in the Founder of Christianity, and is developed throughout the New Testament. A single statement, in addition to what we have already adduced, will bring it again clearly before us: "God hath set the members every one of them in the body, as it hath pleased him. If they were all one member, where were the body? But now are they many members, yet one body. Now ye are the body of Christ, and members in particular."[2]

Both the visible unity of the Jewish state and the spiritual unity of the Christian church were constantly presented to the readers of the Scriptures, and were cherished deeply in the hearts of

[1] Part II., chap. ii., p. 103. [2] 1 Cor. xii. 18–27.

those who laid the foundations of our institutions. Doubtless they exerted a combined and powerful influence on the growth of our national union, which has for its motto "E Pluribus Unum," and the states and citizens of which have been said to be

> "Distinct as the billows and one as the sea."

4. CITIZENSHIP GRANTED TO ALL.

Again it is asked, Whence arose the extension of citizenship to emigrants from all countries?

As the beginning of the answer we must say, It was prompted by the circumstances under which the colonies were planted; but these alone would not have secured it. Men from many nations came hither about the same time—English, Huguenots, Germans, Dutch, Swedes, Scotch and Irish. But how did it happen that these all coalesced harmoniously under English laws, instead of contending with each other perpetually as the Swedes and Dutch did at first, as the English and Dutch did for a time, and the English and French until the latter were subdued?

Not from the Jews was the lesson learned. Among them strangers might attain admission into the commonwealth by embracing Judaism in all its peculiarities; they could also secure a less degree of privilege by a partial conformity. But the main design of the Mosaic dispensation was to separate the Jews, for a time, from other nations, that eventually they might be a blessing to all. Therefore they were a peculiar people, dwelling alone. National prejudice, losing sight of the design of this separation, turned it into a proud exclusiveness, which often refused the most trivial acts of kindness to the people of another race and faith.

Nor from the Greeks was the wisdom derived. They looked on other nations as barbarians, and allowed at best but few privileges to those who came among them.

The Romans, although their policy was in some respects more liberal, granted only an inferior grade of citizenship to people of other lands. It was bestowed partially, capriciously, in different degrees and, in general, at the price of conquest or of gold.

And with reference to the general practice of mankind,

"Lands intersected by a narrow frith
Abhor each other. Mountains interposed
Make enemies of nations who had else,
Like kindred drops, been mingled into one."

Whence, then, arose the American doctrine of citizenship for the people of all countries who come to make this land their home?

We can show a similar doctrine in the New Testament, and think it cannot be traced to any other source. "By revelation," says the apostle of the nations, "God made known to me the mystery (which in other ages was not made known to the sons of men) that the nations should be fellow-heirs, and of the same body and partakers of his promise in Christ by the gospel." "NOW, THEREFORE, YE ARE NO MORE STRANGERS AND FOREIGNERS, BUT FELLOW-CITIZENS WITH THE SAINTS AND OF THE HOUSEHOLD OF GOD." Here we have the source of unity in citizenship.

5. THE ESSENTIAL RIGHTS OF MANKIND.

The American doctrine concerning liberty asserts it to be the equal right of all men.

"We hold these truths to be self-evident, that all men are created equal, that they are endowed by their Creator with certain unalienable rights, and that among these are life, liberty and the pursuit of happiness."

Truths evident now indeed, but are they self-evident? As well might we call the lofty mountain self-evident which, having been concealed during a long night, stands out clearly against the sky when the daylight shines around it.

A doctrine involving these truths was proclaimed in ancient times—proclaimed too at Athens—yet not by Socrates, or Plato, or Aristotle, but by him who on Mars' Hill preached Jesus and the resurrection. "GOD WHO MADE THE WORLD, AND ALL THINGS THEREIN, GIVETH TO ALL LIFE, AND BREATH, AND ALL THINGS, AND HATH MADE OF ONE BLOOD ALL NATIONS OF MEN TO DWELL ON ALL THE FACE OF THE EARTH."

This doctrine underlies the whole fabric of the Scriptures. It was announced at the creation. God said, "Let us make man in our image." It was repeated after the Deluge: "In the image of God made he man." It was celebrated by the song of the angels: "Glory to God, good-will to men." It was confirmed by the Saviour as he approached the cross: "I, if I be lifted up from the earth, will draw all men unto me;" and again from Olivet when he ascended up on high: "Go into all the world and preach the glad tidings to every creature."

Where else can such a doctrine be found, and how, except by revelation, providence and grace, has it been diffused through the public sentiment of the American people? Christianity asserts and maintains the essential rights of mankind.

6. THE STRUGGLE BETWEEN LIBERTY AND SLAVERY.

Not without conflict has the work been done—a conflict between bondage and liberty, between selfishness and the rights of all men, between death and life; a conflict from the first inevitable and incapable of being adjusted except by the triumph of one of the opposing principles and the destruction of the other.

The practice of enslaving the defenceless and the conquered, irrespective of the race to which they belonged and of the religion they professed, is older than history.

By the advancement of Christianity and its attendant civilization it was slowly restricted and undermined. But when it seemed destined to pass away from Christendom it suddenly acquired new force by the substitution of slaves from Africa, inferior, as was supposed, in race, benighted in religion, and barbarous in their modes of life, and consequently, as their enslavers argued, sunk beneath the jurisdiction of Christianity and the compassion of mankind.

"In 1442 some Moors who had been captured

by the Portuguese gave as their ransom, not gold, but *black Moors with curled hair.*" Then a new word came into use and negro slaves into Europe.

This was the little cloud rising out of the sea that was to spread storm and tempest over both hemispheres. From that time the slave-trade began. But at first it did not flourish. Europe furnished no field for the extensive employment of black slaves. It is probable that the traffic would have been abandoned as unprofitable if the discovery of America—the same event which so enlarged the domain of liberty and religion—had not infused into it a vigorous life.

So closely connected in human affairs are good and evil, blessing and cursing. When the paradise is planted the tempter enters; when the sons of God assemble Satan appears; when the seed of the kingdom is sown tares are scattered; when the Saviour's hour of glory comes the prince of this world draws nigh.

This remark applies to the whole continent of America. As soon as it was discovered the work of enslaving its inhabitants began. Columbus himself took hundreds home to Spain, and sold them there. His example was generally followed; and as the natives sank under the burdens thrown on them, it was proposed to take instead of them the more robust negro race.

"The very year in which the Emperor Charles V. sailed with a powerful armament to emancipate Christian slaves in Africa he gave an open, legal sanction to the African slave-trade."

This was the turning of the tide from the slavery of the Old World to that of the New. The trade received a powerful impulse; Spanish, Dutch, Portuguese and British vessels vied with each other in prosecuting it; and at one time, it is said, the sovereigns of England and Spain were the largest slave-merchants in the world.

So it happened that in the English colonies of North America, as well as on more southern soil, the good and the evil entered each upon its course at the beginning.

THE FIRST COLONIAL LEGISLATURE OF VIRGINIA WAS HELD IN 1619.

THE FIRST NEGROES WERE BROUGHT INTO THE JAMES RIVER IN 1620.

THE CULTURE OF COTTON WAS COMMENCED IN 1621.

Thus simultaneously were planted the three germs of the great conflict, liberty, slavery and—cotton, to be exalted as king over both.

In the glance at this conflict which the illustration of our subject has required us to take, we have desired not to look at it from any sectional standpoint or with a biased mind.

We see only our one great country, which God has placed in the midst of the seas, and has given to us. Into it liberty and slavery enter together. They take joint possession not only of the same country, but also of the same human minds and hearts—it is scarcely too much to say of all minds and hearts—of their religious opinions, their social relations, their business affairs, their political plans.

The question to be determined by the conflict between them is, not only whether a portion of mankind are to continue in bondage, but also whether the liberators of the world are to be enslaved. Therefore it is the conflict in its unity at which we look, stretching as it does through two hundred and fifty years, at its small beginning, its expansion, its irrepressibleness, its blood poured out, its treasures lavished, and now at last, by the blessing of God, its end.

It has ended, and Liberty herself is free.

CHAPTER III.

REPUBLICS RESULTING FROM THE PROGRESS OF CHRISTIANITY THROUGHOUT THE WORLD.

Sect. 1.—Republics in Heathen and Mohammedan Lands.

"Many shall run to and fro, and knowledge shall be increased."

(1.) The Rise and Progress of Christian Missions.

WHEN the independence of the United States was acknowledged and the Constitution adopted, the work of modern evangelical missions had scarcely been commenced. The Moravians, with a noble zeal, the English, and perhaps others, had done something to establish Christianity in the European colonial settlements and to spread it among the aborigines around them.

With these slight exceptions, "outside of Christendom there was no recognized preparation, and hardly a visible opening, for the" extension either of the spiritual blessings which Christianity supplies, or of the civilization and liberty which follow in its train.

The Turkish empire had been so far weakened that it could no longer be aggressive against Christian nations, but within its own dominions it was unbroken and apparently strong; was as intolerant as ever in its spirit and as despotic in its sway. The scimitar and bowstring were still its chosen remedies for inquiry in religion and restiveness in the state.

China was closely shut up against the religion, civilization, and even, except at a single port, against the commerce, of Christian lands.

In India, Mohammedan rule had been broken, and the English East India Company, after sanguinary contests, were beginning to consolidate their power. But they were "as anti-Christian in their policy and oppressive in their rule as the Mogul emperor had been."

Africa was shrouded in darkness, and knew Christian nations only as coming to enslave her wretched people, rather than to enlighten and set them free.

Of the islands of the sea, many were yet unknown to civilized nations, some had just been discovered, and all were enveloped in darkness and oppressed by despotic rule.

The modes of traveling from land to land were

slow and the opportunities infrequent. Steam navigation was just beginning to be made a matter of experiment on the waters of the Delaware, the Hudson and the Clyde. Railways were restricted to short distances between coal pits and navigable streams. Locomotives existed only in the minds of the inventors and in their drawings and models. The electric telegraph was so far advanced that a few signals had been transmitted from room to room.

To many minds it may seem only a curious coincidence that, when the people of the United States were establishing their Constitution, a good degree of progress was simultaneously being made toward the accomplishment of these the great inventions of modern times. Of them steam navigation was first in being practically introduced, and the telegraph was last. But in 1789 it would have been difficult to determine which of them would be first completed, while of them all the germs had been secured; and, in point of fact, Fulton's first voyage between New York and Albany, Stephenson's first journey between Liverpool and Manchester, and Morse's first message between Baltimore and Washington, were all realized within a period of thirty-seven years.

Whether the coincidence be called fortuitous or providential, the fact is plain that American republican government, Christian missions, rapid traveling and telegraph communication began their course very nearly at the same time, and are aiding each other in enlightening, liberating and saving the world.

In 1783, William Carey began to agitate the project of sending missions to the heathen, in 1789, it had become the ruling passion of his soul, and in 1792, at his urgent solicitation, the Baptist Missionary Society was formed for the purpose of sending him forth. When he and his companions reached India they were not permitted to remain within the British provinces, but established themselves at Serampore, on Danish soil.

In 1807, Morrison started for China, but was obliged to go by way of America, because the East India Company would not receive missionaries on board their ships, and to set himself down before the gates of the empire, because he could not gain admission within.

In 1812, the first American missionaries reached India, but were ordered by the government to return in the vessel which had brought them. Then commenced, on their part, a series of remonstrances and arguments against the policy of exclusion which gained the attention of Christians in Great Britain. When the subject came before the directors of the India Company, and a resolution was offered requiring the removal of the American missionaries from the British possessions, the venerable Charles Grant, who had been chairman of the court, opposed it, and proved that the government in India had mistaken their duty and assumed unauthorized powers. His argument prevailed, and despatches were sent to Bombay, allowing the Americans to remain. This was the real opening of British India to Christian missions, and not of India only, but also of all the heathen world.

For from that time the zeal of Christians became increasingly earnest and the interposition of Divine Providence increasingly plain; and to-day, after the lapse of only eighty years since Carey advocated the work almost alone, we see that Christianity has been extended by missions and colonies, in a greater or less degree, over the principal heathen and barbarous portions of the globe.

(2.) General Influence of Mission-Work.

In all these enterprises, in whatever land carried forward, numerous schools have been maintained from the commencement of the missions, beginning with those of lowest grade and advancing, as circumstances allowed, to academies, colleges and professional schools.

The Scriptures have been circulated in about two hundred languages and dialects. These include the principal languages spoken in the world. A large portion of the translations have been made by missionaries and their assistants, with great toil, fidelity and skill. Many of the languages had to be reduced to writing before the translation could be made. Much labor, expense and skill has also been devoted to printing the Scriptures. Of this part of the work the British and American Bible societies have done a large share. By the combined efforts of the missions and of the societies many million copies of the whole Bible, or of parts of it, have been circulated in heathen lands.

Hundreds of printing presses have been employed in printing other books, part of which contain practical instruction in religious truth, others being text-books for schools and for students in science and art. The number of printed pages of all kinds circulated among the missions of the American Board alone, exclusive of Bibles printed in this country and Europe, exceeds fourteen hundred millions.

Thousands of preachers proclaim the truth on the Sabbath and during the week to little companies, to crowded congregations, and on favorable occasions to large masses of people. Of these preachers a part are missionaries from Christian lands, and the rest are native helpers and pastors converted and trained for the work.

By such instrumentalities, employed in the principal portions of the heathen world, marked effects on the social and civil condition of the people have been produced and are yet in progress. These effects are similar to those we have already considered in connection with the first diffusion of Christianity, and with its reformation in subsequent times.

A higher estimate is put on human life, the physical and social condition of the people is improved, their mental and moral characters are elevated, religion is gradually separated from the state, and by the wide diffusion of independent Christian churches republics are planted in the midst of despotic governments.

The progress of these results might be exhibited by a particular examination of the whole heathen world, but the work would be in substance a repetition of that which we have already performed. Between the apostolic age and the present the chief difference would be found in the deeper ignorance, degradation and bondage into which the unevangelized nations have sunk with the lapse of time.

(3.) Particular Results.

Instead of continuing longer this general view, we will adduce the results thus far in three countries, which, under widely different circumstances, may be accepted as illustrations of the whole field.

I. The Constitutional Government of the Sandwich Islands.

"Let the multitude of isles be glad thereof."

In 1819 the first company of missionaries for the Sandwich Islands sailed from Boston. On their arrival they found that idolatry had been abolished by the king, and that "the isles were waiting for the law."

The government was of the most despotic and arbitrary character. The people were the slaves of the chiefs, and both chiefs and people the slaves of the king. Whatever property a superior chose to take the inferior must give up; whatever task a superior imposed the inferior must perform. All classes were degraded by superstition, ignorance and vice. The missionaries, in the prosecution of their work, reduced the language to writing, established schools, erected the printing press, translated the Scriptures, organized republican churches and taught the arts of civilized life. By these means the character and condition of the common people were elevated, while the arbitrary power of the rulers was softened and restrained.

In 1840, twenty years after the missionary work began, a remarkable revolution was achieved. The account of it we take from Jarves' History of the Islands, rather than from direct missionary records.

"The king gave his people a constitution. It was a relinquishment of despotic power by the few for the good of the many, not as the result of demands by victorious subjects, but a voluntary change from hereditary despotism and grinding tyranny to written laws and constitutional freedom.

"Not a tittle of the fair scroll was dyed in blood, nor did a threat or a blow urge its execution. The principles of freedom and the knowledge of history pursued at the high-school of the American mission stimulated a spirit of inquiry. Every pupil from that school went forth an unfledged patriot, but in book-knowledge far in advance of his rulers. The wants of the rising generation were not to be bounded by the habits of the old; and, whether against their wills or no, the chiefs were convinced that a change was necessary.

"This was a critical period. But the whole mental and moral influence of the American Protestant mission, itself a most democratic body of a most democratic nation, combined with the advice and example of the most intelligent and influential foreigners, operated to effect a peaceful change. It is no injustice to the foreign traders to attribute this result mainly to missionary efforts. The whole undivided counsels and exertions of the mission have been applied to the spread of Christianity and civilization. How far they have been successful let the result answer. To me it shines like the dawning of the Sun of Righteousness on a blinded race. Even as the oasis engenders life and resuscitates the weary traveler over arid wastes, so these islands redeemed to civilization—the first, if not the fairest fruits of modern philanthropy—foster the toil-worn voyager."

After thirty additional years of faithful labor and of beneficent results, in June, 1870, a jubilee was held commemorating the introduction of Christianity fifty years before. This was an occasion long to be remembered among the islands of the sea, and worthy of profound regard throughout the world.

Flags of all nations adorned the harbor, and happy citizens, in holiday attire, thronged the streets. The king and his ministers, the legislature, the missionaries and native pastors, the diplomatic representatives of foreign nations, with a multitude of people old and young, filled and surrounded the immense church edifice of Honolulu. Of the various addresses delivered there we specify two as most appropriate to our purpose. One was by the minister of foreign affairs, recognizing in behalf of the government the obligations of the people to Christianity, and declaring that their independent government and representative institutions must be ascribed mainly to the teaching of the missionaries and to the civilization introduced by them. The other was by the American minister, fully endorsing the statement, after a knowledge of the islands and of the missionary work extending through forty-five of the fifty years.

II. The Republic of Liberia.

"In the region and shadow of death light is sprung up."

In 1817 the American Colonization Society was formed for the purpose of promoting the voluntary settlement of free colored people on the western coast of Africa.

In 1820 the first company of emigrants was sent out. At the beginning the colony was directed by white men, but many of the settlers, some trained at the North and others in the slaveholding States, were accustomed to the management of their own independent churches, and had acquired some idea of republican government. Consequently, they were soon prepared to assume the management of public affairs.

In 1847, only a quarter of a century after the American flag had been planted on their territory, the Republic of Liberia was formed, having its own legislature, judges and executive. Its constitution is modeled after that of the United States, and by it the independence of religion is secured.

A star of a tropical sky is the emblem on its flag; and not only the emblem of its place among the nations, but also the harbinger of blessedness and light, of peace and truth, to all that vast but hitherto dark land.

In connection with the adjacent British colony of Sierra Leone, Liberia is even now a great blessing to Africa. Two thousand miles of the coast have been delivered from the horrors of the slave-trade, and have received in exchange the benefits of lawful commerce. The republic already includes within its jurisdiction two hundred and fifty thousand native Africans, and is extending its influence into the interior of the country.

In the half century which has elapsed since the founding of the colony many very great difficulties have been overcome, and slavery in the United States, the greatest and apparently most insurmountable obstacle, has been signally removed. Therefore, in the years to come great and glorious results may be expected. Liberia, now a little republic, may be a thousand times enlarged, and grow strong among the nations of the earth.

III. Religious and Civil Liberty in the Turkish Empire.

"*They shall build the old wastes.*"

The roar of battle at Navarino between the allied fleets of Europe and that of the Sultan ceased October 20, 1827, and as the smoke cleared away, Greece was free and the Turkish power broken for ever.

The American missionaries, who were already at work for the enlightenment of the empire at its outposts and distant gates, now reconnoitered it from the Ægean to the Caspian, and in 1831 established themselves in the capital. They translated the Scriptures, conversed concerning the truths of the gospel with all who came to their hired house, preached to the few who ventured attendance, and spread abroad unnumbered printed pages from Greece to Persia.

By these labors the minds of some, especially among the Armenian Christians, were aroused and their hearts affected. They saw the errors of their church and refused compliance. Persecution against them followed; poverty, reproach and anathemas were inflicted on them by their ecclesiastical rulers. This drew forth remonstrance to the Turkish government, and the hand of violence was restrained. Soon after, the Protestants were acknowledged by the government as a religious community owing no subjection to the Armenian church. In 1846, a quarter of a century after "the Bible men" first stood on Turkish soil, a church was formed on the republican model of the New Testament, the first of that description that Constantinople ever saw. In the city where the liberty of the Christian churches had been invaded by imperial patronage, and where Christianity had been overwhelmed by the Turks, there, through the vital energy of the Scriptures, a republican community raised its head in the midst of hierarchical tyranny and of despotic civil rule.

From that time the work has advanced wonderfully throughout the empire. "To-day the Protestantism of Turkey, profoundly interesting in a religious view, has become a political fact of great significance. It is recognized by alarmed and jealous ecclesiastics, it is known in the deliberations of the Sublime Porte and is an element in the international diplomacy of Europe. Turkish Protestants have their charter of incorporation as a civil community, their own internal government, their civil chief and representative at the imperial metropolis. They have become one of the many distinct nations that constitute the empire, religious and ecclesiastical connection being the essence of nationality, and among them all they are distinguished by two characteristics equally American and Christian.

"1. *In that internal self-government which is their chartered privilege they are purely republican.*

Their local officers are chosen by popular election, each local community being a municipal democracy. Their civil chief and his official council at Constantinople are chosen by the united suffrages of all the local communities throughout the empire. Thus they are an organized and chartered republic, with limited powers, under the sovereignty of the Sultan, while in all that empire there is no other rudiment or germ of republicanism.

"2. They have clearly drawn, and persistently maintain, the distinction between church and state, while every other community is recognized and governed simply as a national church through its ecclesiastical officers, its metropolitan bishop being the organ of communication with the imperial government.

"This Protestantism, or, as we might say, this Americanism, is the most vital and growing thing in Turkey. To its converts from the old Christian churches and from the papal sects it is now adding converts from Islamism."[1]

A little while ago it was death to a Turk to change his religion, but now his liberty to do so has been officially declared. Even the great Christian principle of the separation of religion from

[1] Leonard Bacon, D. D.

the state seems about to be applied to the whole empire. Hitherto the Koran has been the declared fountain of authority in both civil and religious affairs. But the Sultan, we are told, has given orders for a separate code of civil law to be prepared. When this is accomplished the Koran will be law only in religion, and for those only who profess the Mohammedan faith.

Sect. 2.—Republican Progress in Europe.

"Wars and rumors of wars, but the end is not yet."

We return again to those countries of Europe where, at the opening of the seventeenth century, amidst gathering storms of war, the struggle was advancing between truth and error, between liberty and arbitrary power.

The bursting of the storm was terrible; the struggle shook Europe and the world. From the destruction of the Spanish Armada to the battles of the Nile and Trafalgar, the roar of the ocean was mingled with the shouts of the victors and the groans of the dying. From the English channel to the Pyramids, and from Gibraltar to Moscow, the land was covered with hostile camps and battlefields and graves.

To the good and evil agencies that were then at

work the influence of America has been added as an assertor of liberty and a dispenser of truth. That influence began when Columbus first saw the light gleam on her shore. It increased when the James River was entered by an English colony, when the Pilgrims landed on Plymouth Rock, and the foundations of Pennsylvania were laid. It was clothed with great power when British statesmen pleaded in her name for the spirit of liberty; when her independence was achieved and her constitution adopted as the supreme law of the land. During seventy years, under that constitution, she became the dread of despots and the hope of the oppressed.

When, in 1861, the "civil war" began, it was hailed with joy by kings, nobles and priests, as if the destruction of popular government was at hand. But in that tremendous conflict the strength of the Republic was proved and the influence of America immeasurably increased.

With this augmented power it is steadily at work on all classes of men, from the sovereign to the serf. It is exerted on government and religion, on literature and science, and on the arts and happiness of social life. It draws away millions from monarchical governments to be citizens of a republic, and these again throw back a reflex influence on their native lands.

The influence of America is exerted by a vast and increasing commerce, by the interchange of millions of letters, transmitted in the swiftest ships and reaching the humblest homes. And now both space and time are conquered: the broad Atlantic no more divides. The sorrows and joys of private life, the course of trade, the decrees of cabinets, the shock of battle, victory, defeat,—all are known instantly and everywhere. On both continents the shout of the multitudes over the fall of despotism at the same moment rends the heavens.

In the midst of such influences let us strive to trace out the progress made toward the establishment of governments of the people over themselves.

(1.) In Great Britain.

"Violence shall no more be heard in thy land."

We begin with England, where, at the time her American colonies were planted, the contest for liberty had been the most successful. But after the death of Cromwell there was a reaction in favor of monarchy. The Stuarts, elated with their apparent triumph and not understanding the spirit of the nation, attempted to renew their arbitrary rule. This produced a second revolution and the call of William and Mary to the throne. Since that time liberty and law have advanced together.

Great progress has been made toward the separation of the church from the state, in the toleration secured to dissenters, in the release of Catholics from disabilities formerly imposed, the voluntary relinquishment of state patronage by the Free Church of Scotland, and the legal disestablishment of the Irish church.

The political power of the people has been extended, partly in a gradual manner almost unobserved, and partly by storms of agitation that have swept over the land.

The country is now, in fact, ruled by the Parliament, and practically, in important matters, the Parliament means "The House of Commons."

If the Peers oppose, they are, in some manner, forced to give up. In every struggle the process becomes easier and the result surer. If in any great crisis, after the voice of the nation had been distinctly uttered by its representatives, the House of Lords should refuse to yield, it would probably be itself swept away.

And as to "the Crown," "that," it has been

lately said, "is the House of Commons." The sovereign, while in theory almost as strong as in earlier times, in practice has scarcely any unrestricted power. He may declare war or peace, but the Parliament controls the purse and the sword. He appoints officers, but the Parliament pays them. Even his appointments are virtually made by the House of Commons; for they are made by the ministers who are selected from its own members, with its consent, are responsible to it and must be changed at its pleasure. The king is said to be capable of doing no wrong and his ministers are responsible for all his acts. But this, in fact, means that he does nothing, the ministers do all.

If, at the present time, it were decidedly the choice of the nation to abolish the royal office, they might do it, we think, with less interruption of affairs than has sometimes occurred between the death of one monarch and the accession of another.

(2.) In France.

"Truth is fallen in the street, and equity cannot enter."

The reigns of Louis XIV. and XV., including their minorities, extended from the English commonwealth to the American Revolution, a period of one hundred and thirty years. The first was distinguished by splendid but exhaustive wars, religious persecution, lavish expenditure and the rigid exercise of despotic power.

Louis XV., by his personal vices, extravagance and tyranny, superadded to the evil consequences of the preceding reign, prepared the way for the overthrow of the monarchy.

It was therefore inevitable that, on the accession of Louis XVI., in 1774, a passionate demand for reform should arise.

The Revolution was hastened by the aid given to the American colonies, by the sympathy felt for their liberty, the influence of their example and the enthusiasm caused by their triumph.

The Constituent Assembly labored to secure civil and religious liberty, equality of rights and popular sovereignty. It overthrew feudal and hierarchical privileges, and tried to establish a constitutional monarchy. The Legislative Assembly, following soon after, abrogated the new form of government and prepared the way for a republic. This the National Convention in its turn proclaimed.

Then commenced the violence and horrors of the Revolution. But for these things—for the cruel murder of the king and his family, of the nobles and multitudes of every rank, for the raging of anarchy, the reign of terror and triumph of military despotism —let no one blame America or republican government. They are all explained by the crusade against the Albigenses, by the massacre of St. Bartholomew's Day and the flight of the Huguenots, which had cut off righteousness and truth from the land and left it a prey to superstition and atheism, to maddening tyranny and brutalizing vice.

After the fall of Napoleon, in 1815, the old dynasty was imposed on the people by the allied powers; but, in 1830, Charles X. was dethroned and Louis Philippe elected "Citizen King." In 1848 a new revolution obliged him to fly hastily out of the country, and the republic was again proclaimed.

Louis Napoleon, nephew of the emperor, and by his will heir to the imperial crown, hastened to France, and by the popularity of his name was elected president. After a solemn oath to uphold the republic he began the work of overturning it. The means by which he became emperor are well known, and need not be recounted here.

For eighteen years he maintained his power, but not without frequent and threatening opposition.

In 1870, feeling that his authority was slipping

away, he professed to renounce his absolute government, appointed a council of ministers and promised larger powers to the legislative assembly. By an appeal to the suffrages of the people he obtained their sanction to his new policy. In this way he secured the semblance of a fresh election, and seemed to expect by means of it to retain the imperial crown and transmit it to his son.

(3.) In Spain.

"She hath no strong rod to be a sceptre to rule."

The patriotic war of the Spanish people against Napoleon rekindled their desire for a liberal government. The Cortes completed a new constitution in 1812, the regency took an oath to support it and the king was invited to resume his reign under it. But, having returned, he declared it null and void, promising, however, to introduce another. Instead of keeping his word, he pursued a despotic course and revived the Inquisition.

In 1820 a military insurrection compelled him to restore the constitution. The press was declared free, the Inquisition was again abolished and the new order of affairs acknowledged throughout Spain. France and other neighboring governments then interfered, with one hundred thousand men, to restore absolute power. Thus sustained, the king revoked the decrees that had been passed under the constitution. Various attempts were afterward made by the people to obtain a larger measure of liberty, but they were suppressed by military force.

In 1868, Queen Isabella was forced to flee out of the country, and a provisional government was declared. By it universal suffrage was ordained and the election of the national Cortes directed. A constitution of a liberal character was adopted, in which religious liberty is secured and the royal office, with limited powers, retained. All efforts, however, to find within the nation a candidate for the crown popular enough to be elected and willing to accept it were unsuccessful, and for two years, with a part of her people openly in favor of a republic, Spain continued to be "a state without a king."

(4.) In Italy.

"Who opposeth and exalteth himself above all that is called God, or is worshiped."

At the readjustment of Europe in 1815 the monarchical institutions of Italy also were restored. The advocates of constitutional government were disappointed, but not subdued. Secret conspiracies were multiplied and many open insurrections made. In 1846, Pius IX., on his accession to the papacy, commenced a reform in the administration of the government, and gave or promised partial liberty of the press and popular representation.

In 1848 the revolution spread through Italy. Rome was captured and the pope obliged to flee. The populace, debased by the falsehoods and tyranny of which they had been the victims for many centuries, hurled after him their malediction, "Fly, thou Jove without thunderbolts! king without crown! apostle without faith!" A republic was then proclaimed and the pope declared to be dethroned from his temporal dominions.

But determined efforts were made by Austria to suppress these popular movements, and, in connection with France and Spain, to reinstate the pope. Rome was resubjected to his sway, and was garrisoned for his protection with French troops.

In 1859, Victor Emanuel was chosen king of Italy, including the whole country except Venetia and the part of the states of the church which the pope still possessed.

A constitutional government has been established and religious toleration secured. The government desires to effect a complete separation of the church from the state. It points to the magnificent spectacle afforded by the United States, and says: "Liberty has produced this; liberty professed and respected by all, in principle and in fact, and in its full application to civil, political and social life. Let us 'render to Cæsar the things that are Cæsar's, and to God the things that are God's,' and peace between church and state will be disturbed no more."

The popular demand was at once for Rome as the natural capital of Italy, but this the presence of French troops kept from them.

Protected by their guns, the pope assembled at Rome, on the 8th of December, 1869, the Catholic prelates of the world to anathematize all this advancement of mankind, and, while his temporal power was trembling beneath his feet, to proclaim him, as the vicegerent of God, absolute master over all temporal and spiritual things.

(5.) In Germany.

"Make our yoke lighter, and we will serve thee."

After the peace of 1815 the suppression of liberal ideas and movements seemed to be the principal object of the Austrian government.

It was foremost in striving to establish arbitrary monarchical rule without any participation by the people.

But its efforts produced reaction and gathered the materials of a popular revolution, which a spark from France, in 1848, kindled into a flame. The monarchy was brought to the verge of ruin. Metternich was compelled to flee and the emperor to abdicate in favor of his son.

The new emperor, surrounded with peril, wisely determined to save his crown by increasing the liberties of his subjects. He entered earnestly on the work, and continued it from year to year, as experience enlarged his conceptions of what he had to do.

At length, in 1865, he pledged to the empire a constitutional government, whose strength should consist in the free participation of its privileges by all the people embraced within it.

This constitution, adopted by the Parliament and approved by the emperor, is now the fundamental law. It is one of the most liberal of Continental Europe, recognizing the equality of all citizens before the law and ensuring freedom of conscience and of religion to every man.

The progress of constitutional government in Prussia, during much of the time under review, so far resembled that in Austria that it need not here be separately considered.

(6.) IN RUSSIA.

"Barbarian, Scythian, bond" and "free."

The history of Russia, confused and turbulent as it has been, exhibits a strenuous conflict between iron-handed despotism and irrepressible freedom.

In 1689, just when William of Orange became king of England, Peter the Great began his reign. Himself a young barbarian of giant strength, great abilities, fierce passions and towering ambition, he fairly represented the empire over which he ruled.

He served among the common soldiers in order to master the military art, worked in the ship-yards of Holland that he might learn how to build a fleet, and went from land to land in search of improvement for himself and his subjects.

By him the germs of Western civilization were planted in his vast dominions. These flourished vigorously during his own and subsequent times.

In 1813 the Russian Bible Society was formed with the sanction of Alexander I. During its continuance the circulation of the Scriptures was prosecuted with great zeal. In 1826 the Society was suppressed by the Emperor Nicholas, but after his death Alexander II. gave permission to resume the work. The Scriptures are translated into the common language of the people, and are widely diffused through the land.

Thus far during Alexander II.'s reign the civilization of the empire has been signally advanced. Thirty-eight millions of serfs have been emancipated by the emperor's decree. Municipal constitutions were given them in connection with their freedom, assistance was furnished them in purchasing the land on which they had been reared and education among them was vigorously begun.

This great work of emancipation kindled a desire throughout Russia for an increase of privileges that would transform the government into a constitutional monarchy. The press expected and began to assume liberty of utterance; the constituent assemblies demanded local self-government and the calling of a general assembly to prepare a constitution.

In partial compliance with these demands, free municipal governments have been given to the large towns and cities, provincial diets have been established and important reforms introduced into the judicial system.

These and similar measures, if faithfully carried out, will mark a new epoch in the history of Russia. They will give her a high rank among civilized nations and inevitably lead to still larger measures of popular liberty.

(7.) General Progress.

"When these things begin to come to pass, lift up your heads."

We have examined separately the progress made toward popular government in different countries of Europe, that we might better understand the work.

But it is not an isolated work. The different countries act and react on each other. By the operations of peace and of war; by the power of a common religion; by trade, commerce and international exhibitions; by lines of railway extending over the continent and thronged with travelers from many lands; by telegrams, ever flashing to and fro and sporting with natural barriers and national bounds,—the people of Europe are being united together.

The waves of Revolution in 1789, 1815, 1830 and 1848 swept over the continent and modified every land. At the present hour " very little of absolute monarchy remains, and an irresistible current drives the people on toward securing greater liberties, and threatens more and more the very existence of kingly rule."

Effects of the Franco-Prussian War on France.

Such was the state of affairs when, in 1870, war was suddenly declared by Louis Napoleon against Prussia on the slightest of pretexts, and even after that pretext had ceased to exist. His real motive, apparently, was by military glory to strengthen his own position and secure the succession for his son, a boy of fourteen.

Seldom have human prospects been more swiftly overcast. In the first important battle the French army was routed; and, after four weeks of unremitted disaster, stripped of all command, the emperor surrendered in person to the king. At Paris, when they knew it, he was instantly dethroned. The insignia of his power were thrown down. The empress regent fled. The empire disappeared, a provisional government was appointed and a republic proclaimed. But, in the presence of the victorious enemy, no opportunity was afforded for an appeal to the people.

The new government was unwilling to ask for peace or to accept it on humiliating terms. The advance of the Prussians was therefore continued and the siege of Paris commenced. Great exertions were made throughout France to repel the invaders, vast armies were organized and sent forth, but they also were soon broken and dispersed. The citizens of Paris were equally heroic in defending their city, and all their efforts were equally in vain. After enduring a siege of more than a hundred and thirty days, in which they were subjected to all the horrors of bombardment and of famine, they surrendered.

An armistice was then granted in order that the National Assembly might be chosen and the question of peace decided. The elections have just been held. All political parties have put forth their strength. But the returns are not in, the results are not declared. Partisans of the Republic, adherents to the dynasty of the "Citizen King," imperialists, are all mingled together in great confusion. The heirs of Louis Philippe come back from their banishment to assert their claims, and Napoleon from his palace prison sends his adroit proclamation as the representative of himself.

In such darkness we may question the telegraph and consult the barometer, but cannot "forecast the storm."

Yet with all our sympathy for the people of France, and all our desire to see a true republic permanently established among them, we must acknowledge that they are poorly prepared to govern themselves.

The best men of the nation having been slain or banished centuries ago, their places were never adequately filled. The word of God has been in a great degree restricted and even proscribed. The masses of the people have been kept in ignorance and error under priestly control. The religious observance of the Sabbath has been almost blotted out. Immorality and vice have been driven from public view in some quarters, and in others have been adorned with splendor and wealth, but everywhere they have corrupted the nation. The imperial government, for eighteen years the centre of power and patronage, was itself founded on perjury and fraud. Therefore, while it did much to suffuse elegance, gayety and mirth over outward things, it could not fail to poison the hidden fountains of national life.

We are now concerned with these facts only so

far as they explain the difficulty of establishing popular government in France. If all efforts to establish it fail, the failure will signally illustrate, from the negative side, the connection between religion and liberty. As the diffusion of the word of God and faith in the pure gospel of Christ tends to soften despotism, to popularize government and establish a republic, so the banishment of the Scriptures and the corruption of the gospel disqualify a people for liberty and subject them to despotism as their inevitable doom.

On the other hand, hope for France may spring from its calamities and sorrow. By being stripped of the fascination of military glory, by being brought low among the nations, by suffering bereavement in myriads of families, by enduring poverty in their homes, the French people may yet find true liberty for this life as well as hope for the life to come. "We have educated the nation for time only" (exclaimed the veteran statesman, Thiers), "and not for eternity; therefore it is not qualified even for the work of time." If, in the depth of their humiliation, the training of the French people for eternity be in truth commenced, if the Scriptures be widely diffused and freedom of faith and practice in religious things be obtained, France may yet be the home of liberty rational and sure.

Amidst the gloom which from our position seems almost unbroken there are some who, standing on a mountain height, think they discern this rifting of the clouds. THE CONCORDAT WITH THE POPE, they tell us, WILL BE ABROGATED, AND RELIGION WILL BE SET FREE.

But if this hope be disappointed, if, with the Scriptures restricted or banished, the priests retain their old dominion over the conscience, whether the government be in name a republic, a monarchy or an empire, the people will still be enslaved.

ON GERMANY.

On the liberties of Germany, what will be the effect of this short but marvelous war?

At first view and for the present it may seem to strengthen the royal prerogative. William left Berlin as king of Prussia: he is now the emperor of Germany, having been crowned in the halls of Versailles. But the victories have been gained by the bravery, intelligence and patriotism of the whole nation of soldiers, rather than by the martial genius of the king and princes. Therefore, while the grandeur of the royal family may be increased and their authority extended over a larger territory, we may still hope that the unity of the German people, and the strengthening of their constitutional liberty, will be important and permanent effects of the war.

On Spain.

During these eventful months, Spain, almost forgotten, has chosen an Italian prince to be her king. He has accepted the crown, has entered the strange land and commenced his reign.

Without attempting to divine his fortunes, we may rest with satisfaction in the belief that at least one great source of national progress and of popular rights has been secured. RELIGIOUS LIBERTY IS ESTABLISHED BY LAW. Every man has guaranteed to him the privilege of reading and obeying the word of God. If this privilege be sacredly maintained and wisely improved, the civil rights of the people will follow surely in its train.

On Italy.

In Italy THE TEMPORAL POWER HAS PASSED AWAY.

Declared the very day—July 18, 1870—on which the infallibility of the pope was proclaimed, one of the first results of the war with

Prussia was the withdrawal of the French troops from Rome. This at once secured the unity of Italy, with its ancient capital restored. The people with one voice required it. Victor Emanuel sent word to the pope that if he should oppose them they would drive him from the throne and proclaim a republic. His troops were therefore ordered to march. They demanded permission to enter the city and were refused. On the 20th of September the attack began, and after a brief contest Rome was free. "The exiles were the first to enter. Leaping the ditches and forcing themselves through the breaches of the walls, they ran to the Capitol to plant there the Italian flag. Their friends gathered around them, shaking them by the hand, embracing them, kissing them again and again. The Romans forgot their stateliness. They laughed, they wept, they clapped their hands, they danced around the soldiers, they shouted for liberty, for Rome, for Italy. The next day, when the general and his officers entered, the tricolor waved everywhere, the houses were crowded to the very top, all vocal with shouts of welcome to the liberators of Rome."

"Surely," says one who witnessed these events, "we are the heirs of all the ages. The breath of those who watched the pomp of the conqueror of Jerusalem streaming beneath his triumphal arch, and of those who saw the honors paid to Pepin when he bestowed the kingdom which has fallen to-day, came not so fast and thick as ours."[1]

With the entrance of French soldiers under Pepin and Charlemagne the temporal power of the popes began, and by the departure of French soldiers it was brought to an end. Yet not by their departure only. As it has been said that the noblest right of the popes at the beginning of their reign was the choice of a free people, so now their power was not wrested from them by the sword alone, but was ended by the almost unanimous vote of the Romans themselves. For, having gained possession of the city, the king commanded his troops to withdraw, leaving the people to choose whether they would remain under the civil government of the pope or would become part of the kingdom of Italy. The vote was taken with entire fairness, as is affirmed by eye-witnesses, and amidst scenes of hilarity and joy exceeding the best days of the carnival. The result has been proclaimed throughout the world: FIFTY FOR THE CONTINUANCE OF THE POPE'S TEMPORAL RULE,

[1] "Lippincott's Magazine," February, 1871.

and FIFTY THOUSAND FOR THE KINGDOM OF ITALY, WITH ITS CAPITAL IN ROME.

In re-united Italy the constitution guarantees the rights of conscience to every man. Romanism and Protestantism are placed side by side without danger of interference or collision. In other words, Europe and the world have one more example of that which we esteem so precious in human government—"a free Church in a free State."

"In this great achievement we discern not only a solace for the sorrows of the past and the fruition of many nobler hopes, but the pledge also of the grandest development in the future. With the rights and liberties of all men secured by the guaranties of a constitutional government; with the state separated from the church, as the essential guard of all political and religious progress; with the sovereign power to control its own destinies, resting within its own borders and among its own citizens,—we are assured that the people of the peninsula will receive a new impulse in all the elements of national life." [1]

But while we rejoice in the fall of the pope's temporal power, let us remember that his spiritual

[1] Address to the people of Italy, adopted in New York, Jan. 12, 1870.

dominion retains its sway over many millions of men, and asserts its claim to absolute and infallible control over all the human race.

With the papacy as a religious system we are concerned directly, in this book, only because from the beginning to the present hour false and idolatrous religion, while it shuts the door of hope against men for the life to come, imposes bondage on them also in this life. Having corrupted Christianity into a mystery of iniquity, the papacy claims to be the sole and infallible possessor and dispenser of Christian truth, and as such the absolute master, in the name of God, over all the world. "*The Catholic Church is the medium and channel through which the will of God is expressed.* THE CHAIN OF COMMUNICATION, COMPOSED OF THE TRIPLE STRAND OF REVELATION, INSPIRATION AND FAITH, STRETCHES UNDERNEATH THE BILLOWS OF ETERNITY TO THE SHORE OF TIME, FROM THE THRONE OF GOD TO THE CHAIR OF ST. PETER; AND THE MIND OF THE SOVEREIGN PONTIFF IS AS CERTAIN TO REFLECT THE MIND AND WILL OF GOD AS THE MIRROR AT ONE END OF THE SUBMARINE CABLE TO INDICATE THE ELECTRIC SIGNAL MADE AT THE OTHER."[1]

[1] Catholic World, July, 1870.

Such is the claim advanced in our day and in free America. As the religion of the Bible and that of the papacy confront each other, the one in the name of Christ, the other as Anti-Christ, so two opposing definitions of religious liberty, going forth from them, stand face to face before the world. According to the one, religious liberty is THE LIBERTY TO WHICH EVERY MAN IS ENTITLED OF DECIDING AND ACTING FOR HIMSELF IN ALL MATTERS PERTAINING TO RELIGION AND TO GOD. According to the other, "RELIGIOUS LIBERTY MUST CONSIST IN THE UNRESTRAINED FREEDOM AND INDEPENDENCE OF THE CHURCH TO TEACH AND GOVERN ALL MEN AND NATIONS, PRINCES AND PEOPLE, RULERS AND RULED, IN ALL THINGS; AND THEREFORE IN THE RECOGNITION AND MAINTENANCE FOR THE CHURCH OF THAT VERY SUPREME AUTHORITY WHICH THE POPES HAVE ALWAYS CLAIMED."[1]

Around these definitions, moral and intellectual, not to say material, forces are assembling in opposing hosts, and the final conflict between them, involving alike the sovereignty of God and the liberty of man, is drawing nigh. Of that conflict we know not the process, the measure or the time,

[1] Catholic World, April, 1870.

but the result we do know. The destruction of the pope's spiritual dominion is as certain in the future as the fall of his temporal rule is now actual in the past.

For of it, Babylon, the great idolatrous and despotic power of the Old Testament, is the New Testament emblem in whose fall its ruin is "signified" by revelation from God. "After these things I saw another angel come down from heaven having great power, and the earth was lightened with his glory. And he cried mightily with a strong voice, saying: 'BABYLON THE GREAT IS FALLEN, IS FALLEN, AND IS BECOME THE HABITATION OF DEVILS, AND THE HOLD OF EVERY FOUL SPIRIT AND A CAGE OF EVERY UNCLEAN AND HATEFUL BIRD.'" "And a mighty angel took up a stone like a great millstone and cast it into the sea, saying: 'THUS WITH VIOLENCE SHALL THAT GREAT CITY BABYLON BE THROWN DOWN AND SHALL BE FOUND NO MORE AT ALL.'"[1]

The course of human history over which we have now passed shows clearly that the revealed truth of God, the centre and life of which is the

[1] Rev. xvii.–xix.

gospel of Christ, while it offers to mankind salvation for the life to come, achieves for them also liberty in this life.

We have given our attention to the latter and secondary result alone, because it is in itself of very great interest and well deserves a more deliberate examination than it commonly receives, because we need to be assured of the connection between the liberty of men and the government of God, and because we thus obtain one of the many demonstrations of the inspiration of the Scriptures and of the divine power of Christianity that can never be overturned, but will increase in strength and brightness from age to age. That which makes this life happy and free is worthy to be trusted for the life to come; that which turns the wilderness beneath our feet into the garden of the Lord will bring us to the promised land.

But though we have separately considered the effects of the Scriptures and of Christianity on this life, let us remember that they never can, in fact, be separated from those which pertain to the life to come. They never can have the first or supreme place. It is only as the Author of eternal life that the Saviour blesses this life. It is only his full and pure gospel which, coming to break the bondage of Satan, breaks also the yoke of despotic power. It is only the direct and earnest endeavor to establish the kingdom of God in the hearts of men that gives them liberty in the state and happiness in the home.

To America as well as to England must Wordsworth's admonition be addressed:

> "Ungrateful country, if thou e'er forget
> The sons who for thy civil rights have bled,
> How, like a Roman, Sidney bowed his head,
> And Russel's milder blood the scaffold wet!
> But these had fallen for profitless regret
> Had not thy holy church her champions bred,
> And claims from other worlds inspirited
> The star of liberty to rise. Nor yet,
> (Grave this within thy heart) if spiritual things
> Be lost through apathy, or scorn, or fear,
> Shalt thou thy humbler franchises support,
> However hardly won or justly dear:
> What came from heaven to heaven by nature clings,
> And if dissever'd thence its course is short."

A word of closer application still remains. While others may so believe and preach and strive for the kingdom of God as to extend the temporal blessings of the gospel to many around them and in distant lands, only by our own personal faith can its eternal blessings be attained. We enjoy the liberty and honor of citizenship on earth mainly through the faith, suffering and work of other men and of other times: let us, by our own faith and acceptance of the offered grace of God, establish our citizenship also in heaven; let us desire the "better country;" let us wait for "the glorious liberty of the children of God."

THE END.

www.ingramcontent.com/pod-product-compliance
Lightning Source LLC
LaVergne TN
LVHW050519100826
845148LV00002B/387

* 9 7 8 1 4 2 5 5 2 0 8 9 2 *